# Perry Mason
# and Philosophy

# Popular Culture and Philosophy® Series Editor: George A. Reisch

VOLUME 1 *Seinfeld and Philosophy: A Book about Everything and Nothing* (2000)

VOLUME 2 *The Simpsons and Philosophy: The D'oh! of Homer* (2001)

VOLUME 3 *The Matrix and Philosophy: Welcome to the Desert of the Real* (2002)

VOLUME 4 *Buffy the Vampire Slayer and Philosophy: Fear and Trembling in Sunnydale* (2003)

VOLUME 9 *Harry Potter and Philosophy: If Aristotle Ran Hogwarts* (2004)

VOLUME 12 *Star Wars and Philosophy: More Powerful than You Can Possibly Imagine* (2005)

VOLUME 13 *Superheroes and Philosophy: Truth, Justice, and the Socratic Way* (2005)

VOLUME 17 *Bob Dylan and Philosophy: It's Alright Ma (I'm Only Thinking)* (2006)

VOLUME 19 *Monty Python and Philosophy: Nudge Nudge, Think Think!* (2006)

VOLUME 30 *Pink Floyd and Philosophy: Careful with that Axiom, Eugene!* (2007)

VOLUME 35 *Star Trek and Philosophy: The Wrath of Kant* (2008)

VOLUME 36 *The Legend of Zelda and Philosophy: I Link Therefore I Am* (2008)

VOLUME 42 *Supervillains and Philosophy: Sometimes Evil Is Its Own Reward* (2009)

VOLUME 49 *Zombies, Vampires, and Philosophy: New Life for the Undead* (2010)

VOLUME 54 *The Onion and Philosophy: Fake News Story True, Alleges Indignant Area Professor* (2010)

VOLUME 55 *Doctor Who and Philosophy: Bigger on the Inside* (2010)

VOLUME 57 *Rush and Philosophy: Heart and Mind United* (2010)

VOLUME 58 *Dexter and Philosophy: Mind over Spatter* (2011)

VOLUME 60 *SpongeBob SquarePants and Philosophy: Soaking Up Secrets Under the Sea!* (2011)

VOLUME 61 *Sherlock Holmes and Philosophy: The Footprints of a Gigantic Mind* (2011)

VOLUME 63 *Philip K. Dick and Philosophy: Do Androids Have Kindred Spirits?* (2011)

VOLUME 64 *The Rolling Stones and Philosophy: It's Just a Thought Away* (2012)

VOLUME 67 *Breaking Bad and Philosophy: Badder Living through Chemistry* (2012) Edited by David R. Koepsell and Robert Arp

VOLUME 68 *The Walking Dead and Philosophy: Zombie Apocalypse Now* (2012) Edited by Wayne Yuen

VOLUME 69 *Curb Your Enthusiasm and Philosophy: Awaken the Social Assassin Within* (2012) Edited by Mark Ralkowski

VOLUME 74 *Planet of the Apes and Philosophy: Great Apes Think Alike* (2013) Edited by John Huss

VOLUME 83 *The Devil and Philosophy: The Nature of His Game* (2014) Edited by Robert Arp

VOLUME 84 *Leonard Cohen and Philosophy: Various Positions* (2014) Edited by Jason Holt

VOLUME 87 *Adventure Time and Philosophy: The Handbook for Heroes* (2015) Edited by Nicolas Michaud

VOLUME 89 *Steve Jobs and Philosophy: For Those Who Think Different* (2015) Edited by Shawn E. Klein

VOLUME 90 *Dracula and Philosophy: Dying to Know* (2015) Edited by Nicolas Michaud and Janelle Pötzsch

VOLUME 91 *It's Always Sunny and Philosophy: The Gang Gets Analyzed* (2015) Edited by Roger Hunt and Robert Arp

VOLUME 92 *Orange Is the New Black and Philosophy: Last Exit from Litchfield* (2015) Edited by Richard Greene and Rachel Robison-Greene

VOLUME 93 *More Doctor Who and Philosophy: Regeneration Time* (2015) Edited by Courtland Lewis and Paula Smithka

VOLUME 94 *Divergent and Philosophy: The Factions of Life* (2016) Edited by Courtland Lewis

VOLUME 95 *Downton Abbey and Philosophy: Thinking in That Manor* (2016) Edited by Adam Barkman and Robert Arp

VOLUME 96 *Hannibal Lecter and Philosophy: The Heart of the Matter* (2016) Edited by Joseph Westfall

VOLUME 97 *The Ultimate Walking Dead and Philosophy: Hungry for More* (2016) Edited by Wayne Yuen

VOLUME 98 *The Princess Bride and Philosophy: Inconceivable!* (2016) Edited by Richard Greene and Rachel Robison-Greene

VOLUME 99 *Louis C.K. and Philosophy: You Don't Get to Be Bored* (2016) Edited by Mark Ralkowski

VOLUME 100 *Batman, Superman, and Philosophy: Badass or Boyscout?* (2016) Edited by Nicolas Michaud

VOLUME 101 *Discworld and Philosophy: Reality Is Not What It Seems* (2016) Edited by Nicolas Michaud

VOLUME 102 *Orphan Black and Philosophy: Grand Theft DNA* (2016) Edited by Richard Greene and Rachel Robison-Greene

VOLUME 103 *David Bowie and Philosophy: Rebel Rebel* (2016) Edited by Theodore G. Ammon

VOLUME 104 *Red Rising and Philosophy: Break the Chains!* (2016) Edited by Courtland Lewis and Kevin McCain

VOLUME 105 *The Ultimate Game of Thrones and Philosophy: You Think or Die* (2017) Edited by Eric J. Silverman and Robert Arp

VOLUME 106 *Peanuts and Philosophy: You're a Wise Man, Charlie Brown!* (2017) Edited by Richard Greene and Rachel Robison-Greene

VOLUME 107 *Deadpool and Philosophy: My Common Sense Is Tingling* (2017) Edited by Nicolas Michaud

VOLUME 108 *The X-Files and Philosophy: The Truth Is In Here* (2017) Edited by Robert Arp

VOLUME 109 *Mr. Robot and Philosophy: Beyond Good and Evil Corp.* (2017) Edited by Richard Greene and Rachel Robison-Greene

VOLUME 110 *Hamilton and Philosophy: Revolutionary Thinking* (2017) Edited by Aaron Rabinowitz and Robert Arp

VOLUME 111 *The Man in the High Castle and Philosophy: Subversive Reports from Another Reality* (2017) Edited by Bruce Krajewski and Joshua Heter

VOLUME 112 *The Americans and Philosophy: Reds in the Bed* (2018) Edited by Robert Arp and Kevin Guilfoy

VOLUME 113 *Jimi Hendrix and Philosophy: Experience Required* (2018) Edited by Theodore G. Ammon

VOLUME 114 *American Horror Story Philosophy: Life Is But a Nightmare* Edited by Richard Greene and Rachel Robison-Greene

VOLUME 115 *Iron Man vs. Captain America and Philosophy: Give Me Liberty or Keep Me Safe* (2018) Edited by Nicolas Michaud and Jessica Watkins

VOLUME 116 *1984 and Philosophy: Is Resistance Futile?* (2018) Edited by Nucci and Stefan Storrie

VOLUME 117 *The Dark Tower and Philosophy* (2019) Edited by Nicolas Michaud and Jacob Thomas May

VOLUME 118 *Scott Adams and Philosophy: A Hole in the Fabric of Reality* (2018) by Daniel Yim, Galen Foresman, and Robert Arp

VOLUME 119 *Twin Peaks and Philosophy: That's Damn Fine Philosophy!* (2018) Edited by Richard Greene and Rachel Robison-Greene

VOLUME 120 *Amy Schumer and Philosophy: Brainwreck!* (2018) Edited by Charlene Elsby and Rob Luzecky

VOLUME 121 *The Twilight Zone and Philosophy: A Dangerous Dimension to Visit* (2019) Edited by Heather L. Rivera and Alexander E. Hooke

VOLUME 122 *Westworld and Philosophy: Mind Equals Blown* (2019) Edited by Richard Greene and Joshua Heter

VOLUME 123 *The Handmaid's Tale and Philosophy: A Womb of One's Own* (2019) Edited by Rachel Robison-Greene

VOLUME 124 *Tom Petty and Philosophy: We Need to Know* (2019) Edited by Randall Auxier and Megan Volpert

VOLUME 125 *Rick and Morty and Philosophy: In the Beginning Was the Squanch* (2019) Edited by Lester C. Abesamis and Wayne Yuen

VOLUME 126 *Stranger Things and Philosophy* (2020) Edited by Jeffrey A. Ewing and Andrew M. Winters

VOLUME 127 *Blade Runner 2049 and Philosophy: This Breaks the World* (2019) Edited by Robin Bunce and Trip McCrossin

VOLUME 128 *Mister Rogers and Philosophy: Wondering through the Neighborhood* (2020) Edited by Eric J. Mohr and Holly K. Baumgartner

VOLUME 129 *RuPaul's Drag Race and Philosophy: Sissy That Thought* (2020) Edited by Hendrik Kempt and Megan Volpert

VOLUME 130 *The Good Place and Philosophy: Get an Afterlife* (2020) Edited by Steven A. Benko and Andrew Pavelich

VOLUME 131 *Avengers Infinity Saga and Philosophy: Go for the Head* (2020) Edited by Robert Arp and Heather L. Rivera

VOLUME 132 *His Dark Materials and Philosophy: Paradox Lost* (2020) Edited by Richard Greene and Rachel Robison-Greene

VOLUME 133 *Perry Mason and Philosophy: The Case of the Awesome Attorney* (2020) Edited by Heather L. Rivera and Robert Arp

IN PREPARATION:

*KISS and Philosophy* (2020) Edited by Courtland Lewis

*Neon Genesis Evangelion and Philosophy* (2021) Edited by Christian Cotton and Andrew M. Winters

*Dave Chappelle and Philosophy* (2021) Edited by Mark Ralkowski

**For full details of all Popular Culture and Philosophy® books, visit www.opencourtbooks.com.**

Popular Culture and Philosophy®

# Perry Mason
# and Philosophy

*The Case of the Awesome Attorney*

EDITED BY

HEATHER L. RIVERA AND

ROBERT ARP

OPEN COURT
Chicago

Volume 133 in the series, Popular Culture and Philosophy®, edited by George A. Reisch

**To find out more about Open Court books, visit our website at www.opencourtbooks.com.**

Open Court Publishing Company is a division of Carus Publishing Company, dba Cricket Media.

Copyright © 2020 by Carus Publishing Company, dba Cricket Media

First printing 2020

All rights reserved. No part of this publication may be reproduced, stored in a retrieval system, or transmitted, in any form or by any means, electronic, mechanical, photocopying, recording, or otherwise, without the prior written permission of the publisher, Open Court Publishing Company, 70 East Lake Street, Suite 800, Chicago, Illinois 60601.

Printed and bound in the United States of America.

*Perry Mason and Philosophy: The Case of the Awesome Attorney*

This book has not been prepared, authorized, or endorsed by the creators or producers of the Perry Mason stories or TV shows.

**ISBN: 978-0-8126-9907-4**

**Library of Congress Control Number: 2020940614**

This book is also available as an e-book (ISBN 978-0-8126-9494-9).

# Contents

Perry Mason, Personification of Objective Truth     vii

## I  *Ethics*     1

1. Is Perry Mason a Good Guy?
   KATHRYN MUYSKENS     3

2. A Paragon of Righteous Virtue
   ROBERT ELLIOTT ALLINSON     11

3. Perry Mason v. Saul Goodman
   FRANK SCALAMBRINO     27

4. The Case of the Other Renegade Refugee
   TRIP MCCROSSIN     35

## II  *Evidence*     47

5. The Case of the Witless Witnesses
   ROBERT ARP     49

6. The Facts Don't Speak for Themselves
   KATHRYN MUYSKENS     63

7. Beyond a Reasonable Doubt
   DOUGLAS JORDAN     75

8. Taking Evidence Personally
   ANTHONY BECKER AND CHARLES TALIAFERRO     81

## III  *Who Is Perry Mason?*     91

9. Perry Mason, Courtroom Messiah
   CHRISTOPHER KETCHAM     93

## Contents

10. Trust and Temptation at the Office
    ALEXANDER E. HOOKE                                107

11. When Is a Lawyer Not a Lawyer?
    JOHN V. KARAVITIS                                 119

12. What about Della Street?
    NOELL BIRONDO                                     133

## IV  Story                                          143

13. *Perry Mason* as Greek Tragedy
    JANET MCCRACKEN                                   145

14. "Yes, I Did It!"
    ALEXANDER E. HOOKE                                157

15. Judge Not, Lest You . . .
    ALEXANDER E. HOOKE                                169

16. Justice: The Master Narrative
    CRAIG R. CHRISTIANSEN                             179

Bibliography                                          189

The Perry Mason Novels and Novelettes                 193

The Classic TV Episodes                               195

Material Witnesses                                    205

Index                                                 209

# Perry Mason, Personification of Objective Truth

ROBERT ARP AND HEATHER L. RIVERA

In 1933 attorney Erle Stanley Gardner first published *The Case of the Velvet Claws*, a story about a lawyer named Perry Mason who was wrapped up in a legal "whodunit" case, the first of eighty-five Masib stories Gardner would write in his lifetime.

Because of these written stories spanning some forty years, three different television series (all of which are shown on TV now as reruns), six theatrical films from the 1930s, a radio series from 1943 to 1955, and an HBO miniseries that premiered on June 21st, 2020, Perry Mason has become one of the most recognized and beloved characters of all time. But why is he so beloved? The answer to this question is actually a philosophically oriented one and, thus, acts as a great introduction to this book.

In the American legal system—which is based on case law and ultimately on constitutional law—it may seem as if the law is something that is not only impartial (consider the number of statues of the blindfolded, scales-toting, sword-wielding Lady Justice that sit in front of courthouses all around the US), but also objective and pure. However, reality dictates that there are all kinds of selfish, error-prone, and even downright evil lawyers, legislators, and jurists who make and enforce bad laws, as well as take advantage of loopholes in good laws. And we all know it. We saw people like O.J. Simpson, Robert Blake, and Casey Anthony beat the rap, all with the help of what many would consider to be "weasel-y" lawyers.

**Robert Arp and Heather L. Rivera**

Yet, we all love a good vindication story. The Innocence Project was founded in 1992 by Peter Neufeld and Barry Scheck at Cardozo School of Law in New York City to exonerate wrongly convicted people in prison primarily through DNA testing, and they have exonerated 367 people since 1989. As of February 2020, a total of 2,551 exonerations have been recorded in the US National Registry of Exonerations. If you have Apple TV, after watching a *Perry Mason* episode on HBO, you can switch channels to Apple's channel to watch the movie *Brian Banks*, which is the inspirational true story of Brian Banks, an All-American high school football star committed to USC who finds his life upended when he is wrongly convicted of a crime he didn't commit. After nearly six years of prison and five years of probation, with the support of the California branch of the Innocence Project, Banks fights to reclaim his life and eventually fulfills his dreams of playing in the NFL with the Atlanta Falcons in 2013. We dare you not to cry at some point while watching this flick . . .

Vindication is what Perry Mason serves up virtually every time he sets foot in the courtroom to defend his client. Whether it's a false accusation, a frame job, or a case of mistaken identity, Perry Mason cuts through all of the baloney and gets at the objective, undeniable truth concerning the matter. And that's what we love about him. And that's what also makes for good philosophical fodder. Philosophers and Perry (P&P) are interested in finding the truth about things. P&P think that there actually is an objective truth "out there" to be found. P&P live for moments of vindication. And P&P think that the law is a transcendent, beautiful thing, wholly unchanging and pure, ultimately *beyond the reach* of not only politicians, advertisers, and mischievous citizens, but also lawyers, legislators, and jurists who can, at times, muck it all up.

Perry Mason is the very personification of objectively true and correct laws. He represents purity, principles, pertinacity, and peaceful human interaction. He's the antithesis of the ambulance chaser. *That's* why we've been reading about him for so many years; *that's* why we have been tuning into our radios to listen to his objections; that's why we have been watching our televisions, as well as going to our theaters, to hear him cross-examine a witness, "So, you're saying you could be *mistaken* about what you say that you saw?"

### Perry Mason, Personification of Objective Truth

These few lines from an anonymous post on Pinterest get at Perry Mason's essence, so before you dive into the truly engaging chapters of this book, we'll leave you with them:

> Perry Mason gave defense lawyers a positive role model. He was no ambulance chaser; people with big troubles rushed to him. I was quite young when my family watched this show, and I recall that his capable secretary, Della Street, and private detective, Paul Drake, helped him be the winningest lawyer on TV! He won because he sought out the truth, no matter where it hid. He wasn't Johnnie Cochran flashy. There was no bull. What a great role model for honesty, the scientific method, and righteousness!

### In Our Memories . . .

We would like to take a moment and remember Barbara Hale; who passed away at the age of ninety-four while the chapters in this book were being written, on January 26th, 2017. Ms. Hale was our beloved Della Street from the *Perry Mason* television series of 271 episodes, and the later thirty TV movies. Barbara captured our hearts and imaginations and will never be forgotten.

# I

# Ethics

# 1
# Is Perry Mason a Good Guy?

KATHRYN MUYSKENS

Perry Mason is the iconic defense attorney, a hero to the wrongly accused. But, is he really a good person?

As the classic television series plays out, Mason's clients always turn out to be innocent, so his personal character or motivation for defending them is never truly called into question. So naturally, like any good philosopher, that's exactly what we're going to do now.

What would it mean for Perry Mason to be a good person? One popular school of ethics is called *consequentialism*—the belief that the rightness of our actions depends on the outcome. This is an attractive theory for many thinkers because, after all, what we really want to know when we ask what's the right thing to do is what will lead to good results.

Mason is a fictional character and throughout the course of the show, despite its many seasons, we learn very little about his personal life outside the courtroom. The only evidence we have to work with is Mason's behavior in the context of his profession. His record there is undeniably spotless. So, if we take a consequentialist view, the answer seems obvious. The outcome of every episode leaves his innocent clients vindicated and the guilty party identified. So, case closed, right? Mason is a good person.

Yet, this can feel like an unsatisfying answer to many people. Consequentialism can answer whether Mason's actions are right or wrong, and might help us choose which actions to take in our own lives. However, what we're interested in when we ask whether someone is a good person is usually not merely the outcome of his past actions. We want to know about what motivates the person, what his character is like. So, what about Mason?

We only get a chance to see Mason's character revealed through the narrow slice of his professional life. This presents us with a unique challenge for gauging his moral character. Since his actions always lead to outcomes we consider good, we're predisposed to think highly of him. Yet, we also must consider that all of those actions are done in the course of his job as a lawyer. It's his duty to defend his clients, no matter whether they are guilty or innocent. Does he really deserve some special moral praise because all the clients he happens to defend turn out to be innocent?

## Doing Good by Chance

One area for trouble in the consequentialist view of morality is the problem of moral luck. Many things that happen in life are due to luck or chance. We're happy to accept that our chances of winning the lottery are a matter of luck. We can buy a ticket, but we know that our involvement stops there. The rest is up to fate. Luck like this is usually not problematic. (Except perhaps when our bad luck leads us to be accused of a murder we didn't commit! How were we supposed to know that the dead body of the guy who was blackmailing us and for whom we just recently declared our hatred would be in the room when the police unexpectedly walk in?)

Yet, when it comes to our own morality, it's particularly disturbing to think the answer might come down to chance. After all, we only know the outcome of our actions once we've done them. But if the outcomes are all that matter in determining whether we're morally praiseworthy or blameworthy, this picture seems at odds with what we intuitively assume about ourselves and others as moral agents.

Immanuel Kant argued that morality is immune to luck. To Kant, the only relevant details in whether someone's actions were moral or not must be within the bounds of that person's control. Outcomes, therefore, are not as important as intentions.

## Is Perry Mason a Good Guy?

Contrary to the consequentialist view, a *deontologist*, like Kant, would argue that certain acts are either right or wrong by their very nature. Crucial to Kant's view is the "good will" or our intent to do the right thing, for the right reasons. Of course, a good outcome, even if unintended, can still be a good thing. But it doesn't make us morally praiseworthy if we didn't do it for the right reason. Similarly, if we had the right intentions, but some factor beyond our control led to a bad outcome, we wouldn't be morally blameworthy, at least not in Kant's view.

Thomas Nagel explored the issue of luck in morality in detail in his article entitled, "Moral Luck." Nagel describes four types of luck that come into play in our moral judgments: circumstantial, constitutive, resultant, and causal. Each type points to an area of life we typically don't have control over.

We don't choose the circumstances into which we are born (circumstantial), we don't choose the experiences that shape us into who we become (constitutive), and much of the time we don't even have control over the effects of our actions (resultant). Nagel's final category, causal luck, comes down to the heart of the free will and determinism debate. If we don't have control over the events that shape and motivate us or the situations we find ourselves in, can we really say we have control over our own actions? Nagel himself seems to be doubtful that we can: "The area of genuine agency, and therefore of legitimate moral judgment, seems to shrink under this scrutiny to an extentionless point" ("Moral Luck").

Looking at it from Nagel's point of view, we may never find a satisfying answer to the question of whether Mason is morally praiseworthy and therefore 'a good person'. But we can still try to uncover some indication of what Mason's intent is in his cases. Would Mason's intent meet the requirements for Kant's 'good will'?

In the world of the *Perry Mason* series, the fates have conspired to ensure that Mason is never in the awkward position of helping the real murderer get away with his or her crimes. However, the fact that Mason's clients are always innocent seems to come down to luck. Most of the time, he has no way of knowing, when they hire him, whether they are guilty or innocent. He simply takes their word for it. Because of his skills as a lawyer, he always succeeds in getting them out of trouble, and happily for everyone involved, uncovers the real killer in the process.

From our privileged position in the audience, we know his client is innocent, not least because (let's be honest) we've probably been watching the show for a while and we noticed a pattern. But what if his client *were* guilty? What would we think of our hero then?

Mason's situation here is special, since as a lawyer he has certain institutional duties to his clients, regardless of their guilt or innocence, that other people wouldn't share. His role in the legal system serves a larger consequentialist good of upholding the function of the justice system, so even if he had to defend a guilty client, it would not necessarily make him a wicked person.

We as viewers, though, would still hope to see evidence of an internal struggle to reassure us of Mason's moral intentions if he were faced with such a scenario. We would want to know that he cares about that consequentialist good, and isn't merely motivated by the money he could earn for his services. This tells us something significant about what we consider important in determining whether someone is morally praiseworthy. Intentions and actions come together to shape our judgment.

Mason's clients are on trial for their suspected *actions*, not their suspected mental states. Yet, motive and character inevitably come into play in the courtroom as reason to believe or disbelieve in their guilt. Likewise, we also judge Mason on his actions in the courtroom, but what we interpret his motives to be shapes our judgment too.

So, which of the following do we take to be a more apt description of his character?

1. Perry Mason only defends innocent people.
2. Perry Mason always ensures justice is done.
3. Perry Mason never loses a case.

All three phrases succeed in summarizing the typical *Perry Mason* episode, but each sentence emphasizes different interpretations of Mason's intentions. What is more important

*Is Perry Mason a Good Guy?*

to him? Is Mason motivated by a competitive urge to win? By an interest in justice? By sympathy for the wrongly accused?

## A Mistaken Confession

In "The Case of the Velvet Claws," Mason's client is the manipulative Eva Belter. From the beginning, she is deceptive and untrustworthy, introducing herself under a false name, Eva Griffin. She gives the viewers and Mason very little reason to trust her.

She comes in originally to enlist Mason in preventing her husband from finding out about an extramarital affair of hers. Her husband happens to be the owner of "Spicy Bits," a gossip magazine. And Eva knows a photo of her with Harrison Burke (an upcoming politician, and her new lover) will soon be published. She tells none of that to Mason, however. He has to find out himself.

Eventually, her husband ends up dead, shot in his office at home. Eva finds the body, and calls Mason before she calls the police. She does everything we would expect a guilty person to do. She lies, tampers with evidence (forging a copy of her husband's will as misdirection), and still Mason does his duty by her as her lawyer. She even coyly accuses Mason of being the murderer! She slyly indicates that her reason for calling Mason first instead of police is because she heard someone upstairs when she found her husband's body. She says, "I'm just sure the man I heard upstairs was you." Mason even gets a confession out of her at one point, and she shouts in his office, "It's true Perry, it's true! It's true. . . . I murdered him, Perry, I murdered him!"

Dramatically, a police detective overhears her confession in Mason's office and walks in just at that moment. Mason seems for the moment to have betrayed his client, by inducing a confession from her knowing a cop would be within earshot. But Mason seems to know something no one else does. Just when it looks as if one of Mason's clients has defied the fates that govern the *Perry Mason* universe, it miraculously turns out that she's innocent anyway! Instead of going immediately to jail, Mason, his client, and the policeman all go to the scene of the crime. Mr. Belter's assistant, Carl, the maid, and Burke are all present in a Miss

Marple-style scene, and Eva recounts her story for all to hear. Somehow, Mason is able to prove that the bullet she fired had missed.

She only *thought* she had shot her husband. In fact, she had missed and someone else came along later and shot him dead. The police overlooked the evidence because the bullet had landed in a pool of water, and the real killer had fished it out later, subsequently shooting Mr. Belter himself.

Mr. Belter's killer turned out to be his own assistant, who saw his chance to take out his boss and the wife (who would inherit the magazine after his death) at the same time. Carl, the real killer, naturally, bursts into tears of confession as Mason explains this to everyone at the scene.

"The Case of the Velvet Claws" is an interesting one because Mason has very little reason to believe his client is innocent. Even *she* thinks she's guilty, for goodness sake! Yet, Mason takes on her case anyway. This seems to indicate that Mason is motivated by his duty as a lawyer, not through prior assurance that his clients are innocent. Yet, when it looks as if she's guilty, for a brief moment Mason acts in a way that looks like he's turning her in, which would be the exact opposite of his lawyerly duty. However, it all works out in the end since it was just a ploy to get her to finally be honest about her role in everything, so that the real killer could be found. Mason's actions then serve the dual purpose of causing justice to be done (the real killer identified), and helping his client avoid a trial for a murder she didn't actually do.

## Perry Mason Loses?

"The Case of the Deadly Verdict" goes down in history as Mason's only loss—sort of. It begins with the end of the trial of Janice Barton, accused of murdering her feeble Aunt Susan for the inheritance money that was coming her way. The jury comes in and announces their verdict: *guilty*! Mason is visibly saddened by the events, and though his client seems resigned to her fate and the other characters, her family, and even Della, are now left wondering if maybe she was really guilty after all, Mason remains firm.

Mason insists she's innocent, and despite the trial being over, he continues to investigate. Eventually, with the help

### Is Perry Mason a Good Guy?

of the police and the family's maid, Mrs. Green, they lure and trap the real criminal by threatening to blackmail him. He is caught when he nearly commits a second murder, attempting to strangle Mrs. Green, whom Mason put up to blackmailing him. The police and Mason are on the scene and step in to apprehend him just before he can do the deed. The act of the attempted second murder is assumed to be a confession to the first. Off screen, this results in Mason's client being set free in the end after all.

The fates of *Perry Mason* just won't let him lose. But, for a while he, and all of us, thought he had. And how he acted in that situation is very revealing of his character. His tenacity on behalf of his client is clearly driven by sympathy and his conviction that she is indeed innocent. He repeatedly declares his faith in her blamelessness. Despite the overturned verdict at the end restoring his perfect record, it's clear that this is not what drives him.

## An Absent Defendant

"The Case of the Terrified Typist" is an even more atypical case for Mason. Mason's client, calling himself Duane Jefferson, is accused of being part of a diamond heist. As it plays out, he is actually *guilty* of the crime, and is about to be convicted when Mason dramatically reveals to the courtroom that his client is not who he claimed to be. His client has been using someone else's name! Mason gets the whole case thrown out as a mistrial. The real Duane Jefferson is an innocent man after all, and the *Perry Mason* universe rights itself by a technicality.

Mason's actions here tiptoe a fine line between legality and morality. He has uncovered the murderer (his own client) and justice can now be done. Yet, in doing that, Mason has been a pretty bad lawyer to his client. He has saved his client from the conviction he was just about to get under one name, but basically ensured his conviction under his real name later. Though unfortunate for pseudo-Duane, the case reveals that Mason's commitment to justice outweighs his sense of duty as a lawyer to his client.

Perry Mason, as he inhabits the universe within the show that bears his name, is fated to always fulfill three criteria:

to win his cases, to vindicate the wrongly accused, and to uncover the real killer. The debate about determinism in our own world may still be raging, but for Mason it's clear there are certain outcomes that will come about no matter what he does. Yet, in a universe where these outcomes are always inevitable, it's not satisfying to us to judge his character solely on that criterion. We want to be assured that Mason's heart is in the right place, too. So, what have we discovered about what drives him?

Mason doesn't defend his clients because he already knows or believes they're innocent, as we can see from "The Case of the Velvet Claws." Eva clearly behaves like a guilty person and even believes she is guilty herself. But, as "The Case of the Terrified Typist" demonstrates, when Mason does conclude his client is guilty, he does something unique. He does something that makes him a pretty bad lawyer for his guilty client, but which furthers the interest of justice. It doesn't even seem that we can say that pride is what motivates him instead of justice. "The Case of the Deadly Verdict" is unique for being Mason's only loss. However, his actions on behalf of his client after the fact show that he is more interested in justice than in his track record. Although, as the laws of the television show universe dictate, as soon as the real killer is discovered, the loss is converted into a mistrial anyway.

It seems as if Mason's values are such that he will sacrifice his duty as a lawyer, even trick or betray his clients, and accept a mistrial in place of a win, all in the interest of justice. Even though the laws of *Perry Mason* have determined that he will always luck out in the end, we can feel confident that Mason's character has the necessary qualities for us to trust that he really is a good guy.

# 2
# A Paragon of Righteous Virtue

ROBERT ELLIOTT ALLINSON

Perry Mason's reputation for skating on the thin edge of legal ethics is summed up by a would be client, Horace Livermore Selkirk, in *The Case of the Deadly Toy* when Horace says to Mason: "You have the reputation of skating right along the thin edge of legal ethics in order to serve your clients. Frequently, your ethics have been questioned, but you have always managed to come up with the right answer and extricate yourself from the difficulty" (p. 85).

Judge Kent in the same story is given lines which speak to Perry Mason's justification for skating on thin legal ice: "As far as this Court is concerned, the primary function of cross-examination is to test the recollection, the skill, and the accuracy of witnesses. Any method, regardless of how unconventional or dramatic that method may be, which tends to bring about the desired object is going to be perfectly permissible in this court. It is far better to resort to the unorthodox and dramatic than it is to have an innocent defendant convicted of crime" (p. 197). Such a statement sums up the legal utopia which Thomas Leitch argues is the reason for the success of the Perry Mason series. This speech aptly sums up Perry Mason's actions and his values. Perry Mason is very nearly an absolute moralist, and has his own Categorical Imperative, the defense of his client. In *The Case of the Singing Skirt*, when resonding to Della, Perry Mason makes it clear that his duty to his client is inviolable:

"... you never wavered in your loyalty to your client, despite the fact that you were virtually certain she had lied to you." ... "Della, ,,, whenever I waver in loyalty to a client ... close up the office, get some paint remover and erase the words ATTORNEY AT LAW from the door of the reception room." (p. 250)

There is no way in which he will betray his client. From this we could infer that Perry Mason is an absolutist when it comes to his code of ethics, but, as we shall see below, Perry Mason's dedication to his own code of ethics, while absolute, also brings difficulties with it when a conflict of duties results in an ethical dilemma. Perry Mason rarely, if ever, is called upon to choose one horn of an ethical dilemma.

## Perry's Ethical Dilemmas

The most interesting example of skating on thin ice is when there is a conflict of duties and Perry Mason finds himself facing an ethical dilemma. An examination of Perry Mason's ethics when faced with an ethical dilemma illustrates that, as Oscar Wilde once quipped when asked during his infamous trial for "the pure and simple truth" answered, "The truth is rarely pure and never simple." The ethical dilemmas, which Perry Mason rarely if ever totally solves, reveal that the philosophical attraction of a Perry Mason murder mystery does not simply lie in its intriguing answers to seemingly impossible questions, but also in the raising of philosophical issues, issues which may not have easy answers, but represent questions with which we must continue to live.

While normally in most detective mystery novels, and *The Case of the Blonde Bonanza* is no exception, the suspense is provided by chasing varied red herrings on the way to the proper solution to the puzzle, what is surprising and fascinating is the role philosophical conundrums play in creating the suspense in Perry Mason crime mysteries. In *The Case of the Blonde Bonanza*, the 'whodunit' is the red herring, while the real mystery to be solved lies in the ethical dilemmas that the case brings to light.

In this sense, the outer shell of the novel, its crime mystery façade, is a lie. It's a lie because the real meaning to be gleaned from the mystery novel is not its ending, the discov-

## A Paragon of Righteous Virtue

ery of the identity of the culprit, but rather in the ethical trials and the responses to the ethical tests that are made along the path. In this sense, the Perry Mason mystery novel is really a philosophical piece, and not only a work of fiction. It is, as Picasso defined art, the lie that tells the truth.

Philosophy begins with rhetoric, with words that arouse our curiosity. In *The Case of the Blonde Bonanza*, what we have is an example of a seemingly lightweight novel, with a title that, tame by today's standards, was probably lurid for its own times. It's a really marvelous example of Aristotle's concept of rhetoric in the service of truth.

And what better means could there be of dispensing philosophy than through a medium so unlikely to be suspected of operating toward this end-goal? The thousands upon thousands of readers, who would turn up their noses at a philosophical treatise on deontological ethics, would eagerly pull *The Case of the Blonde Bonanza* off the bookstore or library shelves and take it home to read. What a delightful surprise to me, as a career professional philosopher, who has taught courses in ethics around the world numberless times, to discover that the attraction that held this reader in suspense in reading *The Case of the Blonde Bonanza* was not only the fascinating mystery plot to be solved, but also the ethical dilemmas and challenges that Perry Mason had to hurdle along the way in order to solve the mystery.

## Sex and Curiosity

Rhetoric shows its hand not only in the title of *The Case of the Blonde Bonanza*, but continues in the use of sexual innuendos throughout the story. Just as in nature, in which sex is used as a lure to procreation, in this work, sex is used as a lure to assist in interesting us, in involving ourselves with the mystery presented. We, like Perry Mason, are in part seduced by the sexual innuendos which are utilized for the purpose of engaging ourselves in the quest to solve the mystery problem, the 'whodunit'. But, rhetoric itself could not work its magic unless it appealed to a curiosity that is inherent in human nature.

In the beginning, Mason's curiosity is aroused by being made aware of a young, buxom, blonde beauty who is of all things trying to fatten herself up. Indeed, this smells fishy to Mason. If Mason did not have the character of being curious and observant, then he would not even have begun this investigation. According to both Socrates and Aristotle, philosophy begins with wonder. Unless we have curiosity about what is going on, philosophy cannot even take off from the ground. Curiosity is a prerequisite for any philosophical investigation.

In this sense, Mason, in *The Case of the Blonde Bonanza*, is led to inquire into what is wrong in the situation by his innate curiosity being aroused. The detective novel and the philosopher have parallel starting points. Mason's reputation for curiosity is indicated in a striking phrase by his confidential secretary Della Street: "I know my boss well enough to know that when his curiosity is once aroused it gnaws at his consciousness like termites in a building" (p. 11).

Perry Mason is, at the same time, an ethical inquirer. He does not want to do anything unethical in his search for truth. Gardner wants the reader to know this at the very start. Early in the novel, when Perry learns that he's invited to a dinner which includes the potential client, Dianne Alder, he wants to make sure first that it is not a trap (p. 10). He does not want to secure a client through any unethical means. In fact, we're tipped off to Mason's ethical bent in the very first paragraph on the first page of *The Case of the Blonde Bonanza* when Della, his secretary, is referred to as his *confidential* secretary. Mason is also described as someone who works hard in the third paragraph of the first page.

## Food and Sex

Gardner does not want to make Perry into a Galahad or a Percival. He also supplies Perry with a good dose of Epicurean traits. In the very first paragraph of the first page of *The Case of the Blonde Bonanza*, his love of food is indicated by the fact that he is heading for a dinner invitation. Mason's curiosity, his capacity for hard work, his reputation for being a hard worker and his interest in food and sex are all combined in the fourth paragraph in the first page: "Any lawyer who gets so busy he regards a Saturday afternoon and a Sunday as being a vacation needs to be taken in hand. Aunt

## A Paragon of Righteous Virtue

Mae has promised one of her chicken and dumpling dinners, the beach will be thronged with bathing beauties, and, I have, moreover, a mystery." Perry's interest in sex is referred to frequently in *The Case of the Blonde Bonanza* (pp. 4, 5, 6, 8, 15, 27, and many others). Mason's character as both virtuous and fun-loving is summed up in the descriptive phrase of Aunt Mae who says to Mason and Della: "You're either talking business or making love and you shouldn't do either on an empty stomach" (p.10). Early on we're told that Mason and his confidential secretary Della are not solely business partners. This parallels Gardner's own life when he married his secretary.

When Mason realizes that the young woman in question, Dianne Alder, may be being taken advantage of by being misled into thinking she is going to be a model for women's clothing that suits overweight females—in fact she's being roped into a contract by which her earnings will be appropriated by the villain of the piece whose surname is Boring—Perry immediately gets down to work. It's apparent that Perry Mason is guided by his sense of justice, by wanting to right what is wrong and at the same time, by a sense of compassion for the innocent victim. The motive of curiosity is augmented by the value of compassion for the intended victim and a desire to do what's right, that is, to right the wrong that is going to be perpetrated if he does not step up to the plate and protect the victim from her wrongful fate.

Added to these two philosophical values is the value of truth-seeking, since Perry is interested in figuring out exactly what is going on. He's interested in finding the reality that lies behind the appearance. The appearance is that his potential client is going on a reverse diet to start a new design trend in women's clothing. As this appearance is suspect, as a philosopher questioning appearances and looking for reality, Perry Mason wants to dig beneath the surface to figure out what's really going on. The desire to know the truth in the situation and to find reality adds to the core philosophical values of curiosity, the righting of wrongs, and compassion.

The importance of Mason's character virtues as motivations for his actions as an attorney are summed up when, after hearing the story of Dianne's contract with Harrison T. Boring (the presenter to her of the weight gaining deal),

Perry Mason says, "This thing has aroused my curiosity. As an attorney I don't like to stand with my hands in my pockets and watch Dianne being taken for a ride" (p. 27). This statement, which combines Mason's philosophical curiosity and his ethical sensitivity, is telling. When he says that he cannot simply stand by and see harm done, this deeply sounds his justice motif. Since the potential victim is an innocent young woman, Mason's compassion is simultaneously stimulated.

## Regardless of Consequences

Perry Mason's justice motif appears to be deontologically motivated. He sees something wrong. He wants to do something about it. There is no utilitarianism in his ethical reaction. He is not motivated because his action will bring about some greater good for society. He is motivated simply because the action that is about to take place is unethical. Deontological ethics, brought into the limelight by Kant in the West and Confucius in the East, is the type of ethics in which the ethical agent acts simply because she or he thinks that she or he must take the right action, regardless of consequences. Utilitarian ethics, as the name implies, holds that the ethical agent acts in order to bring about consequences that are good for people in general. Perry Mason's ethic seems to be a pure Kantian or ancient Confucian one: an ethic that is based purely on doing what is right. The justice motif is sounded explicitly later in the story when Mason says at one point, "I think it's going to be advantageous to take some further steps in the interests of justice" (p. 81). Perry Mason is a modern-day knight (leaning more to a Lancelot than a Percival) in shining armor. He acts to secure justice, nothing else, or so it seems.

We could also understand Perry Mason's ethical reactions from the ethical principles of other traditions. His ethics could be understood from the Jewish concept of *tikun olam*, to repair the world or to rectify the wrongs in the world. His ethical reaction can also be understood as a Buddhist one, a compassion for the suffering of all sentient beings. The importance of compassion as a motivating factor in Mason's ethics is highlighted when the potential victim, Dianne Alder, is described as the sole support of her mother, "who had been helpless for some eighteen months prior to her death. It had taken every cent the girl could earn and scrape together to pay the expenses of nursing" (p. 31). The potential victim and client is vested with an ethical virtue, the virtue of filial piety, a virtue common to both the ancient Confucian and the ancient Hebrew traditions.

Later in the novel, when Dianne who has become his client, and is about to be taken into custody by the police in connection with the murder of Boring, Mason expresses his feelings about the individuals who have tipped off the police to get her involved, "individuals who have played fast and loose with her emotions with absolutely no concern for the outcome" (p. 109). This displays Mason's sense of injustice, that no one should take advantage and harm someone else with no thought to the harm they are doing. That Mason, as is typical of him in numerous Perry Mason novels, takes on this case without fees, reveals another ethical virtue in Mason's quiver of virtues: the ethical value of altruism.

## Compassion and Justice

In *The Case of the Deadly Toy*, Perry Mason springs into action to defend his first client, Norda Allison, a young woman accused of murder, without mentioning a fee. He takes on a second client, a young man who has had his jaw broken with brass knuckles, Nathan Benedict, again without mentioning a fee. In *The Case of the Singing Skirt*, he takes on as a client a young woman and no fee is ever mentioned. In this novel, Perry Mason's attitude about fees is explicitly brought out. He says to his client, "As it happens, Miss Robb, I am primarily interested in the better administration of justice and don't care particularly about fees . . . There will be no charge" (p. 43).

We find other indications of Mason's ethical virtue as the plot of *The Case of the Blonde Bonanza* develops. Another culprit shows his face, a Montrose Foster, the employer of Boring. (A hint that Foster is not the murderer is given by his surname, 'Foster', indicating a foster parent, rather than a real one.) Foster wants to involve Mason in a deal in which he proposes that he, Foster, will do all the work and Mason will receive twenty-five percent as his fee. Mason responds by saying that it's unfair. Here, Mason reveals that his concept of justice requires fairness, anticipating the philosopher John Rawls's celebrated concept of justice as fairness. When Foster replies that Mason has to live, Mason answers, tellingly, "With myself" (p. 55). What kind of ethics is Mason following? Here again, there seems to be an absolutist, Kantian, or Confucian ethics. A person's conscience is the ultimate decider of action in life. There is definitely no self-interest indicated here.

But, as with all ethical motivations, there's another question. When Della asks him if he would be so interested in Dianne's welfare if she were flat-chested, Mason answers, "Frankly, Della, I don't know. But I *think* my motivation at the moment is one of extreme curiosity, plus a desire to give Boring a lesson about picking on credulous young women" (pp. 27–28). What are Mason's true motivations? Here, his answer is two-fold. Firstly, like Socrates, he states that no one really knows what her or his motivations really are, whether we are monsters or whether we are virtuous. This honesty is itself another indicator of Mason's virtuousness. Secondly, he cites two virtuous traits, curiosity and righteousness, one philosophical, the other ethical.

That this problem on which he starts is not the real problem which the text of *The Case of the Blonde Bonanza* centers on, is hinted at in the surname of the initial culprit, Boring. When Boring becomes a murder victim, his name is a clue that even this, the murder that occurs in *The Case of the Blonde Bonanza*, is not actually the central problem. Indeed, compared to what the central problem is, this murder is banal (or boring).

Eventually, as the plot itself thickens, the issues become more complex. What began as a simple problem, becomes a complicated one that contains an ethical dilemma. What begins as an epistemological problem ends as an ethical one. This is the reverse order of Plato's dialogue, the *Meno*, which begins with an ethical question, but then turns into an epistemological one. In the *Meno*, Socrates is asked whether virtue can be taught. He answers that before that question can be answered we must first find out the answer to the question, What is virtue? In *The Case of the Blonde Bonanza*, the question is first, what is really happening here? The ap-

## A Paragon of Righteous Virtue

pearance is of a woman practicing reverse dieting. The question is, What's really the case? In the end, the question transmogrifies into an ethical one: What action should Perry Mason take, as the lawyer for his client, in order to bring about the Good? How should Perry Mason act to prove the innocence of a client who is accused of murder?

The ethical dilemma, which forms the philosophic and ethical crux of this novel, is this. His client, Dianne Alder, is accused of murder. She is the last one seen by an eye witness to be in the presence of the victim (Boring) who is found dead in a hotel room. She claims that the victim was alive and well when she left his room. In order to save her social reputation, another woman, who has been living under the guise of marriage with a man (George Winlock) who is the father of Perry Mason's client, proposes to Perry that to save his client, she will testify that she and her son (Marvin Harvey Palmer) saw the body of the victim drunk and on the floor of the hotel room prior to his client's visiting the room of the victim. In short, she will give false testimony so that Perry's client cannot be prosecuted for the crime. If Perry accepts this offer, he will be suborning perjury. His client will be off the hook, but the price is his committing perjury.

On the other hand, if Perry turns down this offer, he will be confronted with the testimony of the eye witness who swore that the last person to see the murder victim, Boring, was the defendant. Since the body was found dead, and the claimed next to last visitors (Mrs. Winlock and her son) to see the body would claim that he was still alive, Perry's client would doubtless be indicted. In fact, it is revealed that the next to last visitor to see Boring (George Winlock, the father of his client) tells Perry that Boring was alive and well when he left his room, only minutes prior to the time when Dianne went in to see Boring.

Perry considers that the only course of action available to him, as an honest man, is to attempt to impugn the testimony of the penultimate visitor to Boring by bringing up the fact that this visitor was the father of his client. This fact would soften the jury and Perry would get a verdict of manslaughter for his client. This result, if obtained, angers Perry and he exclaims, "To hell with it"—that is, with being ethical.

## A Higher Ethics

The price of being ethical is that Perry Mason's client would get sentenced to life in prison. For Perry, this price is too high. He indicates this when he cries out, "To hell with it"—ethics. This, however, is not a wholesale condemnation of ethics. It's a higher ethics that calls out to him that to be honest to a fault is to follow a lower standard of ethics. On the one hand, Perry can suborn perjury to get his client off the hook: "I have in my hand an opportunity to introduce testimony that will throw the district attorney's case out of the window, get Dianne in the clear, and at the same time get a property settlement for her running into a very substantial figure. If I do that, Winlock—Dianne's father who is another suspect—is going to claim I was guilty of suborning perjury." If Perry does not introduce this testimony, "Dianne is going to get bound over on a murder charge." Perry's best outcome, by not suborning perjury, is that his client is going to be indicted for murder: "That's about the best I can hope to accomplish. That's the price of trying to be ethical. To hell with it" (p. 163).

What Perry means here is that if being honest, and not accepting the offer of perjured testimony, results in the greater wrong of his client's being put away for life, then, the hell with the ethics of lawyers. In other words, while, in the end, the plot of the novel does not require Perry to accept the perjured testimony, and, in fact, on several occasions, he has turned it down, he still feels that the ethics of lawyers, that demands that he turn down the offer of perjured testimony, can go to hell.

What needs to be understood, however, are several important qualifications. While in the text of the novel, Perry Mason *says* ethics can go to hell, he has twice rejected the offer of the perjured testimony, despite the unethical consequences that follow from this. While Perry Mason does not unpack this in the text of the novel, it is legal ethics that can go to hell, not ethics in general. Legal ethics, in this case, seems to run the risk of creating more harm than good. The ethical dilemma still persists. Perry Mason is clearly not happy with the ethical dilemma. This is why he says "to hell with ethics." But, his saying this does not make the ethical dilemma go away.

## A Paragon of Righteous Virtue

Generally, Perry Mason employs all sorts of irregular courtroom tactics, but he does not seem to consider them unethical. He does however, in this novel, consider perjury or suborning perjury to be unethical. While he does not say so explicitly, his behavior by rejecting suborning perjury, indicates that he considers it to be unethical. Now, so far, the entire ethical issue has taken the form of an ethical dilemma. Perry has no solution to it. He simply presents it as an ethical dilemma. As the plot comes to a head, a solution is presented, in a *deus ex machina*, form of the real murderer being identified by Perry Mason. What is interesting here, however, is that Perry has left this ethical dilemma unsolved. Perry does not know how to solve the problem. The problem is *dissolved* by the identification of the murderer, who is not his client; but the ethical dilemma is never actually *solved*.

In situations in which Perry Mason commits irregular acts in the courtroom, we could (and implicitly, Perry Mason did), consider these justifiable means to obtain the end of clearing his innocent client of charges. Perry Mason did not take on the cases of guilty clients. In *The Case of the Deadly Toy*, Perry Mason says, "I always assume my clients are telling the truth" (p. 143). When he considers the possibility of suborning perjury, Perry draws the line (in *The Case of the Blonde Bonanza*). He cannot decide what to do. He cannot decide if he should suborn perjury given the consequences. He says, "To hell with" ethics, because he sees that in the case of an ethical dilemma, there is no ethical solution. This does not mean that we should therefore act unethically. We might take "To hell with ethics" to mean that Perry was teetering on the edge of suborning perjury—but, in the novel, he never has to make this decision (though he has twice turned it down). The point is, ethical dilemmas are not capable of being solved ethically. This is the important point to be made; not to figure out what Perry Mason would have done.

The role of the holder of an unqualified absolutist ethics, a kind of Kantian deontological ethics, in which you do what's right regardless of consequences is given to George Winlock, the father of Perry's client. This suggests that Erle Stanley Gardner considered this position, but was not quite able to make his hero the proponent of it. It may be that it was the author's intent to show the wrongness of such an unqualified absolutist ethics, that he uses this ethical position to illustrate its absurd and harmful consequences.

When the father of Perry's client says that he must be honest, and says that he did see Boring alive and Boring was alive when he left him prior to his daughter's visit to him, it is obvious that he is either sending himself or his daughter to the electric chair, or life imprisonment. His motivation is that he is sick of his life of deceit and he cannot go on with it any more. It is his moral conscience that prompts him into intending to testify honestly despite its horrific consequences. We are reminded of the Kantian prohibition against lying regardless of its consequences. One of the strongest statements in the entire novel is given to this character when he says, "I am going to tell the truth. I've steeped myself in deceit as much as I am going to." And again, "I can't help it, Mr. Mason. I've gone just as far as I'm going to along the slimy path of deceit in this thing. I've got to a point now where I can't sleep, I can't live with myself" (p. 157).

This last quotation, the attribution of a Kantian-like morality to this culprit turned quasi-self-sacrificing hero, reminds us strongly of the exact kind of morality that is characteristic of Perry Mason himself. Truth telling is exalted here at the price of Winlock's own daughter's liberty. This extreme "morality" is both a virtue, and at the same time, absurd. It reminds us of the dilemma that faces the Kantian prohibition against lying under any circumstances. When the Gestapo knocks on the door (in Nazi Germany) and asks if you're hiding a Jewish person in the cellar, according to the prohibition against lying, you must answer truthfully in the event you are sheltering a Jewish person.

The odd vestige of this morality in a semi-villain shows Gardner's ambiguity about the value of absolutist morality, or his wariness that absolutist morality not be misapplied. What is interesting is that Winlock, his name tipping us off that he has the winning hand locked up, eventually does win via his absolutist, Kantian morality. He never does have to testify because Perry discovers the real culprit and makes his testimony unnecessary. At the end of the novel, his interests, not to disclose that he is Dianne's father and hence endanger his current female partner's social position, are served. Could it be that his willingness to be an absolute truth-teller is, in Gardner's eyes, his saving virtue?

## I'll Find Some Other Line of Work

Ultimately, what can we say is the ethical message of the Perry Mason stories? It seems that the message in *The Case of the Blonde Bonanza* is that you should not be an absolutist about ethical rules. On the other hand, Perry Mason is an absolutist in that, in his heart, he places the innocence of his clients over his infraction of the rules of the courtroom. We're left, as we should be, with a question rather than an answer.

What exists, in fact, is a series of ethical dilemmas. In some cases, the ends do justify the means. However, not always. We do not know what to do in the 'not always' cases. Perry Mason does not offer us an answer here. He does his best not to entangle himself in truly unethical means, but it is not shown what he would do if push came to shove. Fortunately, the plot always offers him a way out. Perhaps, that too, is a clue for us.

In *The Case of the Deadly Toy*, in which Perry Mason is investigating whether a young boy has committed a murder, he struggles with a conflict of duties, a true ethical dilemma:

> "My duty is to my client. I can't sit back and let a client take a murder rap simply to spare the feelings of a seven-year-old boy . . . [who would be compelled to testify to his possibly murdering his own father—without testifying, he does not know that he has murdered anyone, only that he has fired a gun in the night]. And yet I can't have that seven-year-old boy dragged up in front of the authorities." (*The Case of the Deadly Toy*, p. 135)

Here, Perry Mason is clearly aware of the ethical dilemma. Needless to say, he eventually finds a solution which does not require the boy's testimony. But the point is that he is actively *struggling* with the ethical dilemma that confronts him. In *The Case of the Singing Skirt*, when Perry Mason has a choice to betray his client to save himself from being disbarred, he says, "I'm not going to throw my client overboard." Della intervenes and says,: "Not even to save your own skin?" Mason shakes his head. Della says, "you'll be disbarred." Mason replies: "All right then . . . I'll find some other line of work. I'm not going to betray a client. That's final" (pp. 217–18). Here, it seems that Mason has solved his ethical dilemma, but in this case it is not a case of hurting another (as with the young boy in *The Case of the Deadly Toy*), but his choice would be to hurt himself which is not the same thing. Mason would seem to make the same choice as Socrates, who famously says that it is better to suffer evil than to commit evil. As usual, in the end, this choice does not have to be made, as the plot works itself out. But, the ethical dilemma (even here where a solution is pointed to), remains as an intriguing philosophical question nevertheless.

*The Case of the Blonde Bonanza*, presents us more with a question than with an answer. It is George Winlock who plays the role of the moral absolutist. He intends to tell the truth regardless of the consequences, whether it endangers his "wife's" social position—he has never married "Mrs. Winlock"—hence this ethical dilemma, like a Russian doll, lies inside an ethical dilemma, his own life or that of his daughter's. In Perry Mason's own case, if he suborns perjured testimony, he can clear his client of a murder charge. If he does not suborn perjury, Dianne will go to trial and most likely be found guilty of manslaughter. In none of these ethical dilemmas do the subjects of the dilemmas get put to the test.

In *The Case of the Mythical Monkeys*, for example, Perry Mason instructs Paul Drake to lock up evidence and Drake protests: "I'm not going to touch that evidence with a ten-foot pole. . . . The stuff is evidence and we've taken into our possession. We're concealing it from the police." At this point Perry hands the evidence to Della (p. 126). Later, as it turns out, this evidence was planted after the police investigation, so holding on to it is not considered illegal action by the judge. But although the story saves Mason from having to take a side in these dilemmas, *they remain ethical dilemmas nevertheless*. Once again, we are left, as we should be, not with philosophical answers, but with philosophical questions.

Perry Mason novels are not, as Randolph Braccialarghe wrote, simply about "the criminal defense lawyer as hero—the indispensable man who proves the innocence of his wrongly accused client." This is the cover story. But, under-

## A Paragon of Righteous Virtue

neath this story is a much more striking ethical lesson. The lesson is that Perry Mason, like all of us, will be faced with ethical dilemmas that may not be resolvable. They may be resolvable, but at terrible price. Whichever way we turn when faced with an ethical dilemma, we have been dealt a losing hand. The real philosophical lesson of a Perry Mason novel is a hard-boiled one, not a Hollywood one. The Perry Mason novels teach us that ultimately there are some contradictions in life with which we must live.[1]

---

[1] The title of this chapter comes from Paul Drake's statement to Perry: "You'll be a paragon of righteous virtue" (*The Case of the Blonde Bonanza*, p. 87).

# 3
# Perry Mason v. Saul Goodman

FRANK SCALAMBRINO

If we compare Season One of *Perry Mason* (1957) with Season One of *Better Call Saul* (2015), we see two TV lawyers hard at work. They both defend their clients with great zeal, they both make a habit of winning their cases, and they both employ somewhat shady tricks to deceive and manipulate the witnesses, the prosecution, and the court. Yet we tend to think of Mason as far more virtuous than Goodman, and as more faithfully serving the ends of Justice.

In order to compare these two quite different lawyers, it helps to consider two quite different philosophies of justice: natural law and legal positivism. Those who believe there is a necessary connection between morality and law tend to support natural law, while those who believe that law is independent of morality—law is just something "posited," as a matter of fact, by people—tend to favor legal positivism. Natural law is often associated with Thomas Aquinas and Immanuel Kant, while legal positivism is associated with Thomas Hobbes and Friedrich Nietzsche.

As Plato famously discussed in the *Republic*, Justice is too great an idea for humans to completely understand in the abstract. However, when we look at what is supposed to be its concrete practical application—for example, regarding some outcome: "Was justice served?"—we do seem to be able to reach agreement much of the time.

## Perry's Problematic Relation to Evidence

Perry Mason tells the court: "My actions, your honor, have been entirely in the interest of Justice" ("The Case of the Crimson Kiss"). When you compare the different characterizations of lawyers personified by Perry Mason and Saul Goodman, you see that Perry is not supposed to be a "villain." However, as was clear to fans of *Breaking Bad* before *Better Call Saul* even appeared, Saul is supposed to be a "shady" character, if not an outright villain. Yet, comparing the first season of *Perry Mason* with that of *Better Call Saul*, at times we witness the protagonists engage in the same type of activity. Thus, we may wonder what different interpretations of justice are contributing to their different characterizations.

Some have described Perry Mason's actions in regard to "evidence switching" as his "trademark" or "signature" style for winning cases—for example, in "The Case of the Crimson Kiss," "The Case of the Runaway Corpse," and "The Case of the Moth-Eaten Mink." Perry does not technically lie to Lieutenant Arthur Tragg. Yet though the Lieutenant's questions do not precisely ask for the information Perry withholds, it's clear to the audience that Perry is omitting information. When Lieutenant Tragg directly asks if Perry had possession of the key to an apartment where a murder took place, Perry answers with a tone of indignation, "You searched me." Of course, Perry's answer doesn't convey what the audience knows to be true.

In fact, in "The Case of the Runaway Corpse" Perry confides in Della Street that he may have "committed a crime" given his relation to the crime scene and questions asked by Lieutenant Tragg. Yet this type of activity is precisely the type of signature activity the audience has come to expect from the character Saul Goodman. And, insofar as the analogy between Della Street and Kim Wexler holds across the shows, when Perry confides in Della, it is as if some unfortunate occurrence has befallen Perry in his pursuit of justice; however, when Saul confides in Kim, it is as if not only his integrity but also the possibility of sanction from the Bar Association is mentioned.

Consider the following episodes involving Perry's potentially problematic relation to evidence. In "The Case of the Crimson Kiss," Perry disposes of an apartment key before the police arrive after he and Della had been in the apartment and discovered a dead body. In "The Case of the Sun Bather's Diary," upon finding out the cash payment he received was with stolen bills, Perry plants one in the blinds of a suspect whom he is not representing. In "The Case of the Restless Redhead" Perry etches grooves into a revolver which was to be counted as evidence in a murder trial. Similarly, in "The Case of the One-Eyed Witness" Perry seemed to be checking the witness's ability to recognize individuals at a distance. However, it turns out to be a trick to get the witness to admit she knows a "parking lot attendant" sitting in the courtroom, and her admission implicates her as complicit to murder.

On the one hand, the philosophical question arises about the unique "omniscient" perspective of the audience. Does such a perspective only have theatrical relevance? If there is no "God's-eye" point of view, then judgments of responsibility or culpability may seem to be based on unfounded evidence. In other words, when Perry is "tampering," so to speak, with evidence, it may be the case that were the audience truly "suspending disbelief," then though the audience is being told the story, in the story no one is witnessing Perry perform these actions. That is, of course, unless there is another character present in the scene.

On the other hand, the philosophical distinction emerges between ends and means; however, this distinction, as we shall see, is further complicated by the distinction between natural law and legal positivism. We might ask, are Perry's actions justified as means to the ends of servicing justice? Of course, one of the more problematic aspects of suggesting the ends justify the means for Perry is that we know at the time he was performing the actions in question he did not know the truth of the situation. That is, he couldn't know ahead of time—as the episodes confirm—whether his client was guilty or not. Rather, like a detective, he seems to be pursuing a "hunch."

## Who Is to Be Master?

It seems reasonable to say that if we believe in a "God's-eye" point of view, then we are in some way and at some time always held accountable for our actions. This is the perspective of morality. Whether it be "karma," "God's justice," or natural physical and psychological consequences, the purview of justice includes even our isolated and solitary actions. Recall, the philosophical distinction between natural law and legal positivism regards the relation between morality and law. Thus, in "The Case of the Restless Redhead" and "The Case of the Sun Bather's Diary," how we judge Perry's "tampering" with evidence should depend in some way on our philosophy of law.

From where does law get its authority? From the natural law perspective, it is as if law were somehow woven into the fabric of nature. Of course, we are a part of nature, and, according to Aristotle humans are naturally "rational animals." Thus, following Aristotle, Aquinas thought of law as *necessarily* a *rational* standard for conduct. This also accounts for the concern of that other great philosopher of natural law, Immanuel Kant, to emphasize the law as universal, and because it is possible to develop an awareness and respect for the necessary and universal aspects of law, Kant understood the law to be unconditional and persons to have a duty to respect it.

In contrast to natural law, legal positivism denies the necessary connection between law and morality. Thus, some associate legal positivism with "convention" and natural law with "nature." In other words, what legitimizes laws and legal systems is that humans have *posited* them. The question that emerges, then, for legal positivism may be characterized by Humpty Dumpty's famous question from Lewis Carroll's *Through the Looking Glass*: "Who is to be Master?"

The classic statement of this relation between law and authority comes from Hobbes. Basically, the idea is that what makes a law is not its content or that it is rational, but rather it is the case that an authoritative power has commanded it. Hobbes refers to this power as one capable of subjecting multiple individuals to its rule by (as Hobbes himself characterized it) "shock and awe." In this way, Nietzsche can characterize law in terms of power, and, perhaps, subsequently characterize morality in the same way. Hence, Nietzsche might say that a court system must discharge its power on offenders; not for the sake of upholding morality, but rather for the sake of sustaining its power as the sole entity authorized to exact revenge.

How does this play out in regard to Perry Mason? We can now examine this question in three ways. First, in regard to the God's-eye point of view, if we take a natural law perspective, we should be tempted to think of Justice in the abstract as a unity that includes both morality and law. In other words, there is just one Justice. Both morality and law are concerned with serving the same Justice. From a natural-law perspective, Perry may be thought culpable for "tampering" with evidence. Second, in regard to the distinction between means and ends, from the perspective of legal positivism Perry seems less culpable for "tampering" with evidence, so long as his actions are "entirely in the interest of Justice."

Because we're examining evidence, it is as if there either is no God's-eye perspective or that perspective does not pertain to legal culpability; therefore, especially since the "evidence" has not yet been officially, that is, legally deemed "evidence," perhaps Perry's "tricks" and "tampering" may be understood as means outside the jurisdiction of legal justice. On the one hand, of course we would need to take into consideration the ethics of lawyering before rendering a judgment. On the other hand, now we can at least see Perry's relation to Lieutenant Tragg with more depth. That is, for example, his omission in "The Case of the Crimson Kiss" may, in fact, be understood as "entirely in the interest of justice."

Finally, by combining the previous two ideas, it becomes possible to think of Perry Mason's actions in terms of gambling in the service of Justice. I will only sketch an outline of this idea here and point readers in a trajectory they can later traverse. Readers may think of Dostoyevski's *Notes from Underground* and the existential implications of envisioning life and, in this case, the pursuit of Justice in the mysterious terms of fate and the probabilistic terms of gambling. The idea is basically that though Perry can choose whether to take a case or pass, he cannot choose what cases become available to him or the circumstances of those cases.

We may be tempted to associate Perry with the philosophy of natural law. For example, episodes with reference to Biblical passages, such as "The Case of the Festive Felon" may be cited as evidence. Further, Perry tends to not just aim for the "reasonable doubt" which could successfully defend his client. Rather, he tends to implicate the truly culpable parties, as if discovering the truth, and the parties in question tend to confess, as if overwhelmed by the weight of the revelation of the truth of their guilt. We see how all this culminates in the "risk taking" captured with the metaphor of "gambling."

If Perry's actions are means serving ends in the interest of Justice, then there is more risk to calculate when he "tampers" with evidence. If the only jurisdiction for justice regarding lawyering procedures, such as those involving evidence, stems from those posited by the Bar and legal authority, then calculating the risk of Perry's actions is different. In the latter case, the material nature of the determining factors seems emphasized. In other words, it may be said that in order for a lawyer to continue to participate in serving the interests of justice, the person must be able to sustain a practice. This doesn't just include financial security but also a tendency to win insofar as that is a factor attracting more business. This is a foundational difference between *Perry Mason* and *Better Call Saul*: the premises of the show make these material concerns moot for Perry. He is already a "rich and famous" lawyer when the series begins.

Hence, notice the following movement between natural law and legal positivism regarding constraints on justice. Though it may be tempting to associate Perry with natural law theory, it's actually from the perspective of legal positivism that we may more easily understand Perry's actions, including those involving evidence, as "entirely in the interest of Justice." The value of this insight is perhaps heightened by comparing Perry further with Saul. For it helps us see how the dynamics of the two shows tempt us to associate Perry with natural law and think of him as in the service of justice, while associating Saul with legal positivism and thinking of him as a villain.

## Truth and the Material Conditions of the Pursuit of Justice

There is a pivotal moment in Season One of *Better Call Saul* in which, after having a million dollars in cash stolen from a family who embezzled it, Saul turns the money over to the authorities. Later, in a parking lot dialog he explains that "whatever it was" that he was listening to which caused him to return the money, he's decided never to listen to it again.

On the one hand, the audience is watching the evolution of the villain-lawyer Saul Goodman from the humorous misguided beginnings of "Slippin'" Jimmy McGill. So, the need for material conditions with which to pursue justice are emphasized if not personified in the lawyer character of Saul. On the other hand, the question which becomes relevant for his comparison with Perry is whether Saul's desire to stop serving "whatever it was" that seemed to previously constrain him with a sense of shock and awe, is entirely in the service of money.

This is not an easy question to answer, since initially we might think that were his actions solely serving money as a kind of master, then he might stop lawyering after obtaining enough money. However, it seems equally reasonable that being in the service of money could mean that he keep lawyering so long as lawyering is his best option to serve money. Of course, as we repeatedly hear about Perry Mason, for example including but not limited to "The Case of the Sun Bather's Diary," "The Case of the Lazy Lover," and "The Case of the Terrified Typist," he's already "rich and famous." Further, if we consider a winning record a material condition to sustain our ability to serve justice, then we have a complicated case on our hands when we consider Saul's "tampering" and "fabricating" in regard to evidence.

After Saul's fateful decision that tempts us to contextualize his philosophy within the purview of legal positivism, he finds himself telling detectives that one of his client's makes "pie sitting" videos, and it was those videos which his client didn't want the police to find, not the alleged prescription pills which the audience knows his client has been selling. Yet, there are no "pie sitting" videos, since Saul made it up on the spot, later he has his client make a pie sitting video which he turned over to the detectives as evidence. When Saul confides this to his analogous Della, Kim chastises Saul and the implication is that his actions were not in the interest of justice.

Thus, finally, we may revisit the question of the characterization of Perry and Saul in regard to the pursuit of

Justice. From the audience's God's-eye point of view, even associating Saul with legal positivism seems to have little effect on diminishing his characterization as a villain. Yet, if we were to think through the movement between natural law and legal positivism regarding Saul, which seemed to provide the best possible justification for the actions of Perry Mason as "entirely in the interest of Justice," then might we change our verdict regarding Saul? At the same time, if we are willing to change our verdict regarding the villain Saul, does this shed anything of a different light on Perry?

## Justice in Question

Of course, Perry Mason always wins, and this coupled with the audience-known fact that his clients are innocent seems to influence how we interpret his relation to "truth," "guilt," "evidence," and "money" in the interest of Justice. Across these two different law dramas, the changing depictions of constraints in the service of justice may receive the majority of their light for audience interpretation from the fact that the former clients are innocent and the latter clients guilty. However, in light of questions regarding the different philosophies of law for these lawyers, we may perhaps have been able to call some of our assumptions regarding Perry's pursuit of Justice into question.

# 4
# The Case of the Other Renegade Refugee

TRIP MCCROSSIN

"One of the top Nazis in Hitler's Germany is in the United States, in Los Angeles, an executive working in your company" under a false identity. So confides Lawrence Vander, a reporter posing as an executive of Space Associates Limited, to Cliff Barlow, the company's Director, in the introductory scene of "The Case of the Renegade Refugee," the thirteenth episode of *Perry Mason*'s fifth season.

We're led to suspect that this "renegade refugee" is the company's Assistant to the Comptroller, Harlan Merrill, who's soon accused of murdering Vander in order to maintain his cover. Convinced of Merrill's innocence, however, and with the assistance of Father Paul, the Superior of the St. Francis Retreat, where Space Associates executives are spending the weekend when the murder occurs, Perry Mason extracts a confession from Arthur Hennings. "My real name is Max Kleinerman," he confesses, even while insisting that he's not Vander's murderer. This distinction, Mason goes on to reveal, belongs to fellow executive, and tawdry adulterer and embezzler, Emery Fillmore.

The most that Merrill's guilty of, it seems, is his own self-described cowardice. As "Lieutenant Philip Kuyper," he confesses, "First Lieutenant, Infantry, 01638166, Army of the United States," in the Battle of the Bulge he "panicked and ran and deserted [his] men and left them [on the battlefield] to die." But as the concluding scene reveals, this too proves to be unfounded. Rather, as a result of the "extreme heroism" he exhibits in attempting to save a wounded Corporal O'Connor, he "suffered shock and concussion in [a] mortar blast."

"When you came to," Mason goes on, "all you could remember was that you'd been running, and in your dazed condition, running meant just one thing," the above panic and desertion. "For more than fifteen years," Father Paul concludes, "you've been living a lie you created in your own mind, paying a debt that didn't even exist. Welcome home, Mr. Philip Kuyper."

The concluding focus is on Kuyper, then, formerly Merrill, the renegade refugee welcomed home. His homecoming is only possible, however, because of the other renegade refugee, Kleinerman, formerly Hennings, his confession in particular. The episode's title suggests that only one of the two must be the storyline's principal focus, and at first blush the former's the better candidate. There's nonetheless a case to be made for the latter, though, if not in the episode's storyline per se, in the broader storyline in which it's set. As the first scene set in Mason's offices concludes, we find that while waiting in the law library, Merrill has consulted a book entitled, *Trials of War Criminals Before the Nuernberg Military Tribunals*. The broader setting, then, is the Holocaust as humanity's most tragic struggle to date with the problem of why the innocent suffer while the wicked thrive, otherwise known as "the problem of evil."

## A Man with a Conscience Is a Man Who Can Be Helped

"Merrill's a funny sort of paradox," Father Paul confides to Mason, explaining what he means by the above. He's "a man who believes he's deeply in debt, knows he can't pay his debt, yet goes on and on hoping to pay it anyway." But while he's "describing a man obsessed with guilt about his past," he's also "not describing a man who is a murderer now." And how could he be, if Merrill's story reminds him of the story of the Retreat's very holy twelfth-century namesake?

This young boy, as Father Paul tells the story, who loved to "laugh and sing," decided one day to go off to war, and did so with considerable fanfare. He fell ill on the way, however, returning home to face humiliation and disgrace as a coward. Praying for guidance in an old dilapidated church, he decided to rebuild it, but in the process compounded his humiliation and disgrace by stealing materials from his father. Still, "in his shame and degradation, the laughing, singing boy—whose name was Francesco Bernardone—found himself," established in turn the Franciscan Order, and was canonized early in the next century as Saint Francis of Assisi.

The reflection of Merrill's story in Saint Francis's confirms for Mason that Merrill is not Vander's murderer, and that the key to proving this is in a bit of information in Father Paul's possession. We know from Barlow's earlier testimony that Vander came to Space Research in the first place because, while searching for Kleinerman in Berlin, he stumbled on a letter he wrote to his late wife. It was a "moving statement by a man who had found for himself at least religious peace of mind," as a result of "a series of talks with a Father Paul." Finally, it was "postmarked the same zone as the St. Francis Retreat," and Space Research executives were the "only organized group at the retreat the weekend of the murder who had been there" prior to the postmark. So Kleinerman must have been posing as one of these executives. But before the weekend of the murder, Mason leads Barlow to realize in his testimony, Merrill had never been to the Retreat, and so can't be Kleinerman.

With Merrill no longer eligible to be Kleinerman, he no longer has any obvious motive to kill Vander, which calls into question Henning's otherwise compelling testimony to this effect. Suspecting already that Hennings is Kleinerman, and that Father Paul must know this as well, knowing him as he does from their "series of talks," and even while not asking him to breach the confidentiality of Kleinerman's confessional, Mason enlists Father Paul in developing a new courtroom strategy. "If I make it clear to this man in court," he asks, of Hennings, who Father Paul has helped to find "at least religious peace of mind," that "his continued silence may cause an innocent man to go to the gas chamber, would he then reveal his true identity?"

In this spirit, the next day in court, Hennings on the stand, Mason asks, "Could there have been certain circumstances, which made it necessary for you to claim that you saw the defendant on the path that night," such that "if

Merrill were guilty, it would have solved a problem for you?" When he resists, Mason appeals to the "at least religious peace" Father Paul has helped him to find. "I'm sure you know this portion of St. Francis's Prayer," Mason offers: "Grant that I may not so much seek to be loved as to love; for it is in giving that we receive; it is in pardoning that we are pardoned; and it is in dying that we are born to eternal life."

"You have the life of Harlan Merrill in your hands," he continues, calling into question again Hennings's testimony that Merrill killed Vander. And here the camera, having recorded the pained look on Hennings's face during Mason's recitation of St. Francis's Prayer, pans down to show him clutching a rosary and crucifix. Ultimately he recants, admitting that Vander was after him, the real Kleinerman, though he's no more guilty of his murder than Merrill. He lied because he "was afraid to face the truth." "I'm not afraid anymore," he confesses, visibly relieved, "I'll take what comes."

The episode's storyline, this portion in particular, is already of no small interest, occurring as it does only a little over a decade and a half after the end of World War II in Europe. So soon after, and a popular television series offers already a redemptive portrayal of a Nazi war criminal. It's all the more interesting, though, in the broader context cited above.

## What's in an Air Date?

*Perry Mason* fans, tuning in on that Saturday, December 9th of 1961, would likely have felt their ears prick up, many of them, upon hearing Vander's initial discussion of "one of the top Nazis in Hitler's Germany." Especially one whose name ends as Kleinerman's does, who the "Allies caught," but who subsequently "escaped." After all, one such "top Nazi" had been in the news of late: Adolf Eichmann.

Eichmann had escaped an Allied detention camp in January of 1946, and fled to Argentina in 1950, as Ricardo Klement, but had finally been captured relatively recently, on May 11th of 1960, by agents of the Israel Security Agency, Shin Bet, and removed to Israel nine days later to stand trial. Controversy over these actions grew in subsequent months, so much so that in August, it reached the United Nations Security Council, which resolved in the end that Ar-

## The Case of the Other Renegade Refugee

gentina's sovereignty had been violated and that it was owed reparations. And they remained sufficiently controversial throughout the following Autumn and Winter to justify a feature film, *Operation Eichmann*, chronicling Eichmann's crimes, flight, and capture, which appeared on March 15th of 1961, just shy of a month before Eichmann's trial began.

## A Man without a Conscience

*Operation Eichmann*, a "docufiction" in the current vernacular, filmed in black-and-white to give it the unmistakable feel of a documentary, has many of the hallmarks of being rushed into production, presumably in order to capitalize on, though hopefully also to reflect sincerely the importance of paying attention to history as it's unfolding. It's nonetheless a remarkable document, though, most notably for its conspicuously fictional first minute or so. The only bit of genuine artistry in the movie, it's a telling snapshot of the public's perception of Eichmann, or so its writer and director, Lester Cole and R.G. Springsteen, must have imagined.

The screen is shrouded in darkness, but for a light shining down from the top left portion of the screen, on Eichmann speaking from the docket. As the camera slowly moves in on him, a drum roll slowly building to a crescendo, he chillingly dresses down those who have tried and sentenced him.

> Justice. Justice! Who are you to speak of justice? All of you out there, staring at me, as if I were an inhuman monster, a grotesque beast. You there, smug and self-satisfied, now that I have been captured. You will learn of true justice. And you will get it. *From us!* Even now, at this moment, while I stand here, forced to perform in your circus, your travesty of a trial, we are rising again, once more growing in strength, in Germany, in Argentina, in America. You will put me to death, but you will stop nothing. Hang me, but watch. As you spring the trap on the gallows, look at my dangling feet, and you will see them dancing above the millions I have sent to their graves. *Heil Hitler!*

The drum roll reaches its crescendo, ominous music follows, the title and credits roll, and a narrator, David, who we meet again halfway through the film as the leader and moral compass of Operation Eichmann, introduces himself. "I am one of the survivors of the hell and holocaust that was Nazism," we learn. "Even now," he goes on, "so many years later, I still must remind myself that Adolf Eichmann was not only a beast and grotesque monster, but the final end product of a political process. Adolf Eichmann was a Nazi." Cue the chronicle of Eichmann's crimes and capture, allowing David to confront his tormenter finally in the film's concluding scene. "I regret nothing," Eichmann boasts, "I do not repent. *Kill me!*" But David, who has steadfastly resisted such expediency and satisfaction, has other plans.

> That's too easy, too quick. You're going to stand trial, Eichmann. People are going to see you. They're going to study you. They're going to learn how one man can become responsible for the torture and murder of six million human beings—*six million!* The world will learn, and they'll *remember!*

Against the backdrop of David's stirring lead-in, Eichmann's trial begins just shy of a month later, on April 11th of 1961, lasting a little over four well-publicized months, ending on August 14th. When "The Case of the Renegade Refugee" went on air four months later, on December 9th, roughly a third of the way through Season Five, the anticipated verdict was only a few days away, on December 12th, his death sentence pronounced only a few days later, on December 15th. Only a few days after the season's finale on May 26th of 1962, after a roughly six-month appeal process in the wake of sentencing, and a little over a year after his capture, Eichmann was hanged shortly after midnight on June 1st.

As David had hoped, as a result of evidence presented at trial from nearly eight months of taped police interrogation, from May 29th of 1960 to January 17th of 1961, and from Eichmann's own statements and demeanor there and upon execution, people did see and study him. And from their seeing and studying—some of it more symbolic, some of it more factual—we learned to struggle to understand.

On the more symbolic front, we have "The Case of the Renegade Refugee." The *Perry Mason* series as a whole was the first hour-long serial crime drama, with unusually high-quality production and a "reputation among writers as being the hardest one in Hollywood to work for" (*Writer's Digest*, 1961). It seems likely, then, even though we've no public record to this effect, that Samuel Newman developed the storyline and wrote the script during the trial and its aftermath, especially given the episode's storyline, and the fact that it's one of only two episodes to deal directly with warfare, and the only one to address World War II and Nazi atrocities in particular.

It seems just as likely that the writing process took into account the pursuit and capture that preceded it, given the inclusion of Vander's long and circuitous hunt for Kleinerman. If so, it's reasonable to imagine that Newman was also, consciously or unconsciously, aware of and reacting to *Operation Eichmann*. In so doing, he offers a competing interpretation of "the final end product of a political process," even one as heinous as Nazism, which includes the likes of Eichmann—the recalcitrant guilt denier who relishes his mass murder—but *also* of Hennings/Kleinerman—the reluctant acceptor who's prepared to "take what comes."

## Neither Monstrous, Nor Repentant, But . . .

On the more literal front, one seer, studier, and teacher stands out: Hannah Arendt, most famously for *Eichmann in Jerusalem*. It appeared in May of 1963, as a result of her reporting on the trial for *The New Yorker*, in which it appeared beforehand in five installments in February and March. It is, according to Susan Neiman's *Evil in Modern Thought*, "the twentieth century's most important philosophical contribution to the problem of evil," doing more than any other to help us to *see* and, as David also hoped, *remember* Eichmann.

There are certain similarities, some of them eerily prescient, between the artfully frightening first minute of *Operation Eichmann* and Arendt's report. "Bragging was the vice that was Eichmann's undoing," she reports early on, and in particular there's the example she gives. "I will jump into my grave laughing," he boasted, "because the fact that I have the death of five million Jews on my conscience gives me extraordinary satisfaction." This can't help but recall the film's introductory invective, but the recollection is nonetheless tempered by her earlier description of Eichmann. He was "the man in the glass booth built for his protection," after all, "modium sized, slender, middle-aged, with receding hair, ill-fitting teeth, and nearsighted eyes, who throughout the trial keeps craning his scraggy neck toward the bench."

Likewise, there are similarities with Hennings's testimony in "The Case of the Renegade Refugee." "After a short while, gentlemen, we shall all meet again," Eichmann uttered shortly before he's hanged, as "is the fate of all men," reminiscent of the "at least religious peace" Father Paul helped Hennings to find. This too can't help but be tempered by Eichmann turning away the Protestant minister on hand before his execution, on the grounds that "he had only two more hours to live, and therefore no 'time to waste'." It's also tempered by what Hennings's "religious peace" allows him to do, which is to reveal himself as Kleinerman, with all the peril that that would have to entail, in order to save Merrill. Worse than the bragging, that is, Arendt reports, "a more specific, and also more decisive, flaw in Eichmann's character was his almost total inability ever to look at anything from the other fellow's point of view." The empathy clearly written into Hennings/Kleinerman is just as clearly absent in Eichmann on trial.

In spite of similarities, then, the perspective on Eichmann that Arendt presents is importantly distinct both from the Eichmann of *Operation Eichmann* and from Hennings/Kleinerman in "The Case of the Renegade Refugee." This is no more evident than in the idea, ever controversial, with which she closes the principal text of *Eichmann in Jerusalem*. The "lesson that this long course in human wickedness has taught us," she concludes, speaking of Eichmann's trial and execution, is "the lesson of the fearsome, word-and-thought-defying banality of evil," the turn of phrase becoming the book's provocative subtitle, in its post-periodical form: *A Report on the Banality of Evil*.

What's lost in the subtitle, however eye-catching, is a subtlety found in the text. It's not so much that the personification of evil may be surprisingly banal, that is, which is hard to deny in comparing Eichmann at trial with the "beast and grotesque monster" of *Operation Eichmann*. It's also, and more importantly, that its development in the world is the "end product of a political process" of a broader sort: the fear-

## The Case of the Other Renegade Refugee

some, and all too common, defiance of language and thought—fearsome because it surely leads to a defiance of others, a denial of their natures, of their existence even, that's equally so.

"The longer one listened to him," Arendt tells us, "the more obvious it became that his inability to speak was closely connected with an inability to think, namely, to think from the standpoint of somebody else." It was impossible to communicate with him "not because he lied, but because he was surrounded by the most reliable of all safeguards against the words and the presence of others, and hence against reality as such." Reflecting back some years later, in 1972, on the controversy that developed immediately in response *Eichmann in Jerusalem*, Arendt stood by its central contention.

> Some years ago, reporting the trial of Eichmann in Jerusalem, I spoke of "the banality of evil" and meant with this no theory or doctrine but something quite factual, the phenomenon of evil deeds, committed on a gigantic scale, which could not be traced to any particularity of wickedness, pathology, or ideological conviction in the doer, whose only personal distinction was a perhaps extraordinary shallowness. However monstrous the deeds were, the doer was neither monstrous nor demonic, and the only specific characteristic one could detect in his past as well as in his behavior during the trial and the preceding police examination was something entirely negative: it was not stupidity but a curious, quite authentic inability to think.

Still, the controversy persists to this day, both in academic circles and in more popular media, though perhaps without quite the ferocity of its first few years. As Mary McCarthy wrote in a letter to Arendt four months later, in September of 1963, the fierce nature of the backlash was, she thought, "assuming the proportions of a pogrom." It would have been very difficult indeed, then, if possible at all, for anyone to ignore it who was thinking about World War II in the months leading up to September 17th, 1965.

## Again, What's in an Air Date?

Film, television, and philosophy conspire to offer us three different perspectives—the grotesquely monstrous Eichmann of *Operation Eichmann*, the confessional and repentant Hennings/Kleinerman of "The Case of the Renegade Refugee," and the unrepentant, but banal Eichmann of *Eichmann in Jerusalem*. That the controversy regarding the latter persists is perhaps testimony enough that the choice itself still resonates in popular culture.

Its resonance is made more problematic, however, by the shock we might have felt, if familiar with *Operation Eichmann*, tuning in to CBS four years later, on September 17th, 1965. Airing that evening was the pilot episode of a new television series, also filmed in black and white, with the provocative tag line, "If you liked World War II, you'll love *Hogan's Heroes!*"

It opens with the view from above, as a military-style drum beat pulses, of what appears to be a POW camp, with "Germany 1942," in large Gothic script, splashing across the center of the screen within a few seconds. Cut then to searchlights in guard towers panning back and forth, a boot kicking open a door, and prisoners filing hurriedly out, shown impersonally only from the waist down, in wintertime, judging from the snow on the ground.

Cut again, roughly twenty seconds in, to one barracks in particular, where a German officer, who would have to have looked familiar, more lazily urging those within to exit, which they do in a manner distinctly less hurried. And cut yet again, just shy of half a minute in now, to a building labeled "Kommandantur," from which emerges another German officer, clearly the other's more distinguished superior, who would also have to have looked familiar, all the more so for being paired with the other.

"Good grief," we might have blurted out, in response to these apparent look-alikes, "that's *Eichmann*, and that was *Höss* a moment ago, the first of his henchman we hear from after *Operation Eichmann*'s introductory monologue . . . they're on *television* . . . in *prime time* no less . . . what in the *world?*" And how could this not be confirmed as the title and initial credits splash across the screen moments later, and the actors who portrayed Eichmann and Höss in *Operation Eichmann*, Werner Klemperer and John Banner respectively, are confirmed to be the Kommandant and underling who've just impressed us. Perhaps *Hogan's Heroes* is the story, we might have thought, of what Eichmann and Höss were doing shortly before the famous Wannsee Conference in January 1942—to be forgiven, of course, for forgetting that *Operation Eichmann*'s timeline begins with a meeting Eichmann called in 1941.

Doubt would soon have crept in, though, as the first post credits scene unfolds, in which prisoners are referring to Höss as Schulz, and then, as we're coming to grips with this, we hear a laugh track. "*Eichmann*, though maybe not Höss . . . in a *situation comedy* . . . what in the *world?*" But, of course, it's not to be, as we learn finally, toward the end of the third scene, just shy of ten minutes in, that it's not Kommandant Eichmann, but Kommandant Klink, and that *Hogan's Heroes* is indeed a situation comedy set in a German Prisoner of War camp so incompetently run that it's been infiltrated by a band of faux-POWs, led by Colonel Hogan. *What in the world?*

## What to Look for When History Repeats Itself

It would be uncharitable to think that the creators of *Hogan's Heroes*, Bernard Fein and Albert Ruddy, would have been unaware of their provocation in choosing Klemperer and Banner, who'd played Eichmann and Höss only four years earlier, to play Klink and Schultz. They may not, however, have anticipated how the spirit of the provocation would play out over time. In spite of the series running for fully six seasons, that is, through April of 1971, and securing for Klemperer Primetime Emmy Awards in 1968 and 1969, for "Outstanding Continued Performance by an Actor in a Supporting Role in a Series," the show came to be seen as among our least finest pop-culture moments. By 2002, that is, the series was designated the fifth worst in *TV Guide's 50 Worst TV Shows Ever*, at least in part for the slight it reflected to World War II prisoners of war and, albeit less directly, victims and survivors of the Holocaust.

History repeats itself twice, someone very clever once said, first as tragedy and then as farce. But what if it does so, in some instances at least, in order to force us to look again at what lies in between? In this case, what's traditionally thought to lie there is Arendt's rightly famous account of how fearsomely, all the more so for how banally, we allow ourselves to let go of thinking and empathy as our most effective tonics against not only suffering the likes of Eichmann, but *becoming* his like.

What "The Case of the Renegade Refugee" provides, and in particular the example of the *other* renegade refugee, Hennings/Kleinerman, is a welcome complication of what lies between. Between the demonic and the farcical, we see and remember, thanks to Arendt, a "beast and grotesque monster" who's banally unrepentant, but against the background now, thanks to Newman, of one who, albeit fictional, is believably repentant, even while no less banally so.

By the end of the summer of 1961, after months at trial, preceded by months of interrogation, producing thousands of pages of transcript, Israeli Attorney General Gideon Hausner, the chief prosecutor at Eichmann's trial, was unable to wrest from him, as Arendt reports, any thoughtful and empathetic repentance. By the end of the year, however, Mason had been able, as Newman writes him, to wrest from Hennings/Kleinerman precisely this.

Art resisting life, so that life may later imitate it. We hope.[1]

---

[1] I'd like to thank Sue Zemka and her trusted companion, Fergus, for giving me the space and encouragement to finish this. I'm grateful to Sue in particular for her happy observation that I'm channeling here Marx's enduringly clever view of history. I'd also like to thank the folks in my "Problem of Evil in Philosophy and Popular Culture" seminars in the Honors Program and Byrne First-year Seminar Program at Rutgers University, during the Fall semester of 2016, for their helpful ideas, and Honors Program, Honors College, and Byrne Seminar Program Deans, Administrative Deans, Assistant Deans, Directors, Administrative Directors, and Adminstrative Assistants Vanessa Coleman, Paul Gilmore, Jennifer Jones, Muffin Lord, Matt Matsuda, Angela Mullis, and Julio Nazario, for making it possible for me to conduct them. Finally, I'd like to thank this volume's editors, for patience and understanding far and away above the call.

# II

# Evidence

# 5
# The Case of the Witless Witnesses

ROBERT ARP

> There is almost nothing more convincing than a live human being who takes the stand, points a finger at the defendant, and says, "That's the one!"
> —Former US Supreme Court Justice WILLIAM J. BRENNAN, JR.

> PERRY MASON: My client is telling the truth when she says she was nowhere near the scene of the crime . . .
>
> HAMILTON BURGER: Well, Perry, we have someone who saw the whole thing . . . We have an eyewitness!

I've been playing the drums since I was a kid, and the first time I performed with a rock band for an audience, it was inside the gym of a Catholic grade school for a fundraiser when I was sixteen. It was memorable not only because it was my first taste of what it's like to get several people to bang their heads to the admittedly loud heavy metal music I played with my band Noble Savage, but also because about halfway through our set the chair of the fundraiser got sick of the "noise" and decided to pull the plug, literally. I recall watching Mr. Chairman walk over to the side of the stage and the next thing you know, the guitarists were attempting to shred their axes, but no sound was coming out of their Marshall stacks.

The whole thing was recorded on VHS video by my dad, who had a choice seat above the crowd in the back of the gym. Boy, were we pissed! The lead guitarist threw his guitar down on the stage, we all stormed off exit stage left, and our bass player started hollering at Mr. Chairman until Fr. O'Malley had to intervene, ending the night on a total downer. Over the next few days, I told the story to my friends and family about how this jerk pulled the plug. The next weekend, I decided to sit down and watch the video of the show. Here's the funny thing: I remembered vividly in my mind that Mr. Chairman walked over and pulled the plug, but in the video it was actually the *wife of* Mr. Chairman who can be seen doing the deed. "Huh," I thought to himself when I saw her pulling the plug in the video, "I could have sworn it was Mr. Jerky Chairman Jerk."

I bet something like this has happened to you as well, where you're absolutely convinced that you remember some event, or some person, or some object being a certain way, but then come to find out you were wrong, and you're surprised because you had convinced yourself that your memory was correct. Now, imagine cases where you never know you were incorrect about your memory, and it's your memory of an event that can mean the difference between life and death for someone, like in courtroom criminal cases.

That happens all of the time, apparently, and the Innocence Project—which was founded in 1992 by Peter Neufeld and Barry Scheck at Cardozo School of Law in New York City to exonerate wrongly convicted people in prison principally through DNA testing—claims that, of the 367 exonerees since 1989, 28 percent of them have involved false confessions, 44 percent involved misapplication of forensic science, and a whopping 69 percent of them have involved some kind of eyewitness *mis*identification. Of that 69 percent, 35 percent had to do with incorrectly identifying someone in a lineup, 52 percent with misidentifying people in photos, 32 percent with misidentifying the same person by different witnesses, 85 percent with misidentification by a surviving victim, 54 percent with an in-court misidentification, and there are other reasons for misidentification, as well as other reasons for why these people were wrongly convicted (https://www.innocenceproject.org/dna-exonerations-in-the-united-states/).

Can you imagine going to prison, or even being sentenced to death, because an eyewitness mistook you for another person, the actual criminal?! Think about those poor folks exonerated through the Innocent Project *before* they were exonerated. It's a triple whammy: you got the sentence you're serving in prison, which is horrible enough psychologically, physically, and spiritually; you got the anger, frustration, and helplessness surrounding the knowledge that they "got the wrong guy" and there's probably nothing you can do about it as you sit there in your jail cell; and you got the injustice of the real criminal still out there on the streets likely committing more crimes, when s/he should be sitting where you are. What a soul-crushing and utterly depressing nightmare that would be!

## That Man Sitting There

There are few things more compelling than a witness pointing out a defendant in the courtroom as the "one who did it"—that's why I started this chapter with the two quotations from Justice Brennan and the fictitious LA County DA, Hamilton Burger, from Erle Stanley Gardner's *Perry Mason* stories. There are several episodes of the *Perry Mason* TV series that I watched on my little black-and-white TV growing up where the witness on the stand would declare, "That's him!" pointing out the defendant in the courtroom (for example, "The Case of Constant Doyle," and "The Case of the One-Eyed Witness"). According to the numerous citations found in Robert Norris's *Exonerated: A History of the Innocence Movement* (New York University Press, 2017) as well as the citations from the papers found in *Wrongful Convictions and the DNA Revolution: Twenty-Five Years of Freeing the Innocent* (Cambridge University Press, 2017), edited by Daniel Medwed, the criminal justice system in the US—and the systems in many other countries of the world—recognizes that eyewitness testimony in general and eyewitness identification in particular are key to capturing, prosecuting, and sentencing criminals. The cops rely heavily on eyewitness testimony in their initial investigation of a crime, while eyewitness identifications from lineups and photo spreads happen all of the time. And the eyewitness is probably the single most common form of witness in many criminal trials.

In fact, when I went to serve jury duty a few years back in Johnson County, Kansas, as I walked into the courtroom the bailiff handed me a brochure from the Johnson County Administrative Office of the Courts called "Common Courtroom Phrases and Questions." In it, besides examples of what you might hear on an episode of *Perry Mason* like, "You may be seated," "You may proceed," and "Will the defendant please rise," there was this exchange, meant to demonstrate a typical line of questioning from an attorney to a witness:

> ATTORNEY: Do you see the man you saw holding the 9 mm pistol in this courtroom?
>
> WITNESS: Yes.
>
> ATTORNEY: Can you point him out?
>
> WITNESS: Yes. That man sitting there.
>
> ATTORNEY: Let the record show that the witness has identified the defendant.

On the face of it, it makes sense that eyewitness reports provide strong evidence in criminal cases because people generally believe that the way in which a person recalls an event must directly correlate with the way the event actually happened. It's as if the mind and our memories are thought of as a camera-video recording process where the camera of our senses records in real time when an event is occurring in front of us, stores it on the blank tape of the mind in our memories for an indefinite amount of time, and then can be played back, at any point, when we're recalling that event and telling someone else. And the "playback" or memory of the event is assumed to *accurately* match up with, or *correctly* correspond directly with, what actually happened.

## Lousy Recorders

Unfortunately, as numerous experiments and research into perception and memory have shown over the past fifty years, or so, our minds and memories are lousy recorders. So while it may be that few things are more convincing than a witness pointing and saying, "That's him" in a courtroom, few things are also more unreliable than eyewitness testimony. Just as I was certain it was Mr. Chairman who pulled the plug on my

## The Case of the Witless Witnesses

rock band—and, to this day, I still have the image of him, and no one else, walking toward the outlet—yet I was incorrect in my memory of the event, so too people will say, "I'll never forget *that* face" or "There's no doubt in my mind—it was *that* guy" about people in line-ups or defendants in courtrooms, and later they are stunned to find out they were wrong.

It's kind of like the way the Chief of Police of Oceanside, California, felt after being cross-examined by Perry Mason in *The Case of the Dubious Bridegroom*. The Chief was shaken by Mason's recreation of the events surrounding tire tracks at a crime scene because *before* Mason's intense series of questions he recalled events one way, but *after* Mason's barrage he admits he was wrong about his recollection:

> PERRY MASON: You say the only way that you knew the car was left waiting there was because the tracks curved?
>
> CHIEF OF POLICE: Well, the car was waiting there. You could tell by the way the tracks were of the car where the murdered woman was found . . .
>
> PERRY MASON: Just what was there in the tracks of this car to show you that it had been left waiting?
>
> CHIEF OF POLICE: Well, you could see where the tracks of Ethel Garvin's car had been manipulated around to get in just the right position.
>
> PERRY MASON: Then it wasn't anything in the tracks of the car that had been left waiting that showed you what had happened, but something you'd deduced from the tracks of an entirely different automobile.
>
> CHIEF OF POLICE: Well, if you want to put it that way, yes . . .
>
> PERRY MASON: You're doing the putting . . . but kindly try and put it right.
>
> CHIEF OF POLICE: Well, that's the way it was.
>
> PERRY MASON: Then you were mistaken when you said you could tell from the tracks of the getaway car that it had been left waiting there?
>
> CHIEF OF POLICE: No, you could tell it from the tracks like I explained to you.

**PERRY MASON:** But what was there about the tracks of the car that had been left waiting that showed it had stood there?

**CHIEF OF POLICE:** Well, it—well, you could see from the way the other car had been sidled up to it . . .

**PERRY MASON:** Was there anything in the tracks of the car that you say had been left waiting there that showed it had been left waiting—in the tracks of that one particular car?

**CHIEF OF POLICE:** Naturally there couldn't be. You can't tell from car tracks whether a car just drove in and then went right out, or whether it stopped for an hour, or two hours, or four hours, unless you had some change in condition, such as a rainstorm while the car was parked there or something.

**PERRY MASON:** Oh . . . then you were mistaken in stating to the jury when you gave your testimony on direct exanimation that the tracks of the parked car showed it had been left there for a while?

**CHIEF OF POLICE:** Sure . . .

**PERRY MASON:** So you were mistaken?

**CHIEF OF POLICE:** Well, I . . . I guess so.

**PERRY MASON:** I knew you were . . . I just wanted to see how difficult it would be to make you admit it. That's all, Chief . . .

"The vagaries of eyewitness identification are well known," Former Supreme Court Justice Brennan wrote in an important case affirming a defendant's right to counsel during pre-trial lineups back in 1967, *United States v Wade*, "the annals of criminal law are rife with instances of mistaken identification."

That is what happened in the case of Richard Phillips, who spent forty-six years in prison for a murder he didn't commit. An eyewitness swore Phillips committed the cold-blooded act back in 1971, and he was sentenced to Michigan's death row. In 2017, DNA evidence exonerated Phillips, who currently holds the record as the "longest-serving innocent man in the US," a title I'm sure he doesn't get all gushy about. Kirk Bloodsworth spent two years on death row in a Maryland prison for a rape and murder of a nine-year-old girl he didn't commit, largely on the basis of mistaken eyewitness testimony. Like Phillips, Bloodsworth was later exonerated by DNA evidence, and he holds the title of "first person sentenced to death in the US to be exonerated by DNA testing after conviction."

Connecticut and Massachusetts have already limited the use of the in-courtroom "That man sitting there" approach. In both states, the main concern has been that the witness in the courtroom was making the identification for the first time, and hadn't previously picked the defendant out of a standard lineup or photo array. And in several cases the witness was making a courtroom identification weeks, months, and even years after the crime took place! A 2016 decision in Connecticut's Supreme Court held that witnesses can't be asked for an in-court identification unless they knew the defendant before witnessing the crime or have already successfully identified the defendant in an out-of-court procedure, or the perpetrator's identity is not at all contested. Since 2014, Massachusetts's Supreme Court has banned in-courtroom identifications, unless it can be shown that the witness was absolutely *and unequivocally* certain in identifying the defendant *before* the trial.

We could fill several volumes with cases from recorded history of people wrongly convicted because of mistaken identification. Of course, people have been wrongly convicted for other reasons, such as a witness lying, police or others tampering with evidence, and even framing people, set-ups, and prejudice on the part of judge or jury. The high-pressure, nerve-racking environment surrounding law enforcement questioning and other activities can also lead to a witness misidentifying someone. In *The Case of the Dubious Bridegroom*, Perry Mason asks the witness who was instrumental in fingering the suspect, "Did the officers use a line-up so that there were several men in your line of vision and then ask you to pick out the man you had seen?" The witness replies, "No, sir, they didn't. There was just this one man there . . ." Now, we could easily see how that *one man* was *the man* to be arrested for the crime. That's straightforward police bias and corruption!

But we're talking about legitimate, innocent, honest-to-goodness mistaken identification on the part of an eyewitness here. How does *that* happen so frequently? How do we make sense of these mental mistakes, these memory mishaps, these recall rejects? Why is it that, at times, we can be such lousy recorders of events, people's faces, or objects in the world?

## Memory = Recall of Experience + Added Information

Since the early 1970s, Elizabeth Loftus at the University of Washington has been recognized as one of the most important researchers of memory, especially in relation to eyewitness testimony of all types. In her groundbreaking work, now in its sixth edition, titled *Eyewitness Testimony*, Loftus and her two colleagues, James Doyle and Karen Newirth, demonstrate that when we recall events that we've experienced, our memories of the events don't accurately match up with what actually happened. Instead, what is recalled is a *reconstruction* of the actual event with all kinds of extra ideas, images, and pieces of information added. In other words, Memory = Recall of Experience + Added Information.

So, unlike a recorded tape getting played back any number of times that shows the exact same video over and over again, our memories are more fluid, malleable, and changeable over time. In fact, if you've ever played the "telephone game"—where Person A whispers a few sentences that describe some event into the ear of Person B, then Person B has to repeat the same thing into the ear of Person C, and so on—if you compare the actual, original few-lined story to the account given by the tenth person who tells the tale, the story has changed dramatically. I've used the following a number of times for icebreakers and to demonstrate the evolution of oral tradition while teaching: "Team B is playing Tennis before Team A tonight, while Team A is playing volleyball. Let's get on the bus. It's a long way to San Francisco through San Jose." I urge you to try it with several people, and see how much the story changes from Person A to the last Person.

In a study done by Dutch researchers, ten months after El Al Flight 1862, a Boeing 747 cargo aircraft, crashed into apartments in Amsterdam on October 4th, 1992, participants were asked if they recalled seeing the TV footage of the plane hitting the building on the news. Sixty percent reported that they'd seen it and were able to fill in details such as the angle of the plane as it hit the structure, the fireball that was created, and even the sight of the inside of half the fuselage for a moment before it exploded. The problem was there was no TV footage! These people were making it up, without knowing they were doing so, probably based on information they heard from news and other people. When that sixty percent were eventually told that there was no TV footage, all were shocked, some cried, some became angry, and some refused to believe that the Dutch researchers were telling them the truth. One participant said, "That can't be true. I *saw* the plane hit. I *saw* it." Another went so far as to claim, "I would have sworn on the eyes of my mother that there was news footage of that airplane hitting the apartments."

## In a Flash

Loftus and her team have performed numerous experiments and studies demonstrating that memories are reconstructions of events with pieces of information added, just like the Dutch El Al Flight 1862 study. Even more remarkable is a lengthy study performed by Ulric Neisser and his colleagues relating to the 1986 *Challenger* disaster. In *Memory Observed*, Neisser explains how he asked some of his Psych 101 students to document where they were when the space shuttle *Challenger* exploded on January 28th, 1986. Seventy-three seconds after liftoff, a seal failed on the *Challenger*, and the vessel blew up into a ball of fire, sending plumes of smoke out into a Y-shaped entanglement that took three times as long to fall back to Earth. Anyone who watched live coverage on TV realized immediately that something had gone horribly wrong, and the tragedy was definitely etched into their minds (I was just about to turn sixteen at the time, and I recall the horror and sadness surrounding the event).

Neisser questioned the same group of students several times throughout the spring semester of 1986 about where they were and what they were doing when the *Challenger* exploded, then again a year and a half later, then three years later. "When I first heard about the explosion, I was sitting in my freshman dorm room with my roommate and we were watching TV. It came on as a news flash and we were both totally shocked," wrote one of the students in June of 1987. However, just twenty-four hours after the disaster, that same student had written, "I was in my religion class and some people walked in and started talking about it. I didn't know any details except that it had exploded and the schoolteacher's students had all been watching, which I thought was so sad." This was one of forty-four students in the study and, according to Neisser, there was a marked difference in the accounts of *all* forty-four students between their responses in the twenty-four-hour time period, the year-and-a-half time period, and the three-year time period after the *Challenger* disaster.

Recalling such an emotionally charged event like the *Challenger* disaster is an example of a *flashbulb memory*, a term coined back in 1977 by Harvard psychologists Roger Brown and James Kulik. I know people who still can recall where they were when JFK was assassinated in Dallas on November 22, 1963, or where they were glued to TV sets or radios when "the Eagle has landed" on the Moon and Neil Armstrong took, "one small step for a man, one giant leap for mankind" on July 20, 1969. I recall vividly where I was when my wife called me to tell me, "Turn on the news. An airplane hit the World Trade Center" on 9/11/2001. Just like anyone else describing a flashbulb memory, I can recall a number of details about the environment I was in, what I was wearing, and who was with me at the time. And just like anyone else, *to me* it all seems completely accurate, even though it may not be, in the same way that the one participant in the Amsterdam study really believed he "*saw* the plane hit. I *saw* it," and simply couldn't believe the researchers when they revealed the fact that there was no TV footage of the plane hitting the building.

## I *Thought* His Face Rang a Bell . . .

Research on flashbulb memories is showing that our recollections—incorrect as they are, at times—also remain extremely coherent, vivid, and certainly real to us, which leads to this conclusion: emotionally charged events don't necessarily create accurate memories, but they do necessarily seem to create in us the conviction that our memories are

## The Case of the Witless Witnesses

accurate. Perry Mason notices this kind of confidence in Howard Scanlon, one of the witnesses in *The Case of the Dubious Bridegroom* (p. 156):

> "Just the same," Mason said, "there's something about that witness that bothers me. He's prejudiced, he's testifying to a composite of what he thinks he saw, what he thinks he remembered, and what he thinks must have happened, and he's now testifying positively; but somehow there's a certain underlying sincerity, a rugged sense of fairness the guy has that bothers me."

But the fact that emotionally charged events *don't necessarily* create accurate memories seems all wrong and counterintuitive, doesn't it? You would think that some kind of huge event, such as a life-or-death situation, would make a *lasting impression* on your mind. "I'll never forget that face for as long as I live" is a mantra that can be heard on video, and read about in reports, from victims who have survived after being robbed at gunpoint, raped, or shot and left for dead, for example. It might seem that the more intense the situation, the more indelible the memory of a person's face, or what they were wearing, or the car they drove, would be in a victim's memory. But in fact the most emotionally charged events can be remembered very inaccurately.

We can understand this counterintuitive phenomenon in light of something called the Yerkes-Dodson Law, which describes a bell-shaped relationship between arousal/excitement and performance/activity. When your mind (or body) is aroused, it performs better, and here there seems to be a solid correlation between the two. In fact, we can trace that performance from the base of one side of the bell up to the top of the bell, with increase in performance matching increase in arousal. But then performance not only plateaus—at the so-called top of the bell—but it starts to decrease as it heads down to the base of the other side of the bell! So, if you get *too* excited or aroused, you make mistakes, you get tired out, and your performance decreases. In other words, victims of crimes might be *too* stimulated with fear to remember an assailant's face, clothing, shoes, or car accurately.

In *Eyewitness Testimony*, Loftus, Doyle, and Newirth talk about a study of military students at a US survival school performed by psychologist Charles Morgan, III, where soldiers are placed into traumatic combat situations that are as close to reality as is possible, such as being deprived of food and sleep, shot at, gassed, soaked excessively with water, as well as experiencing heat, cold, loud music, and other nasty experiences over an extended period of time. The idea, of course, is to get soldiers used to what they may experience in actual combat.

More than five hundred soldiers participated in the study, which focused on the part of training having to do with being captured by the enemy and interrogated by three interrogators over an hour-long period. There were two groups: a group of soldiers experiencing *low-stress* interrogation with joking, refreshments, and friendly questions; and a group experiencing *high-stress* interrogation, complete with emotional, psychological, and even a bit of physical hostility. After the event, each soldier was shown an array of nine pictures that included a picture of one of the interrogators, was told that just one of the interrogators is among the array, and was asked to identify the interrogator. The low-stress group had a 76 percent success rate of identifying an interrogator, while the high-stress group had a 34 percent success rate.

Morgan concludes, "These data provide robust evidence that eyewitness memory for persons encountered during events that are personally relevant, highly stressful, and realistic in nature may be subject to substantial error." This finding seems to support the Yerkes-Dodson Law, and explains the numerous cases recounted by the Innocent Project of how it is that several women who experienced the horror of being raped for many minutes, could still either not identify their rapists in line-ups, or misidentified the rapists, mistakes which often contributed to sending innocent persons to prison.

## A Paradox

Traditionally, murder mysteries have assumed that eyewitness testimony is infallible, and part of the appeal of such stories has to do with the author setting out a puzzle for the reader. Erle Stanley Gardner is no different, in this respect. But where Gardner *is* distinguishable from the typical murder mystery writer has to do not only with the nitpicky kinds

## The Case of the Witless Witnesses

of questions that Perry Mason asks in the courtroom that frustrate his witnesses, as well as the so-called *Perry Mason moment* (where evidence or other information is introduced in the courtroom unexpectedly and the case takes a dramatic turn toward the opposite outcome—a rare occurrence in the real world), but also the fact that he is able to demonstrate time and time again that a witness is mistaken about what they perceived and/or what they remember.

When Erle Stanley Gardner had Perry Mason discount, discredit, and dog eyewitness testimony in his pre–World War II stories, this was actually something kind of new. As a seasoned defense lawyer in 1930s Los Angeles, Gardner was fully aware of how inaccurate eyewitness testimony could be, and he wrote this awareness into many of his stories. It was only later, with the work of Loftus in the 1970s, that psychologists, neuroscientists, and others began studying memory and eyewitness testimony under rigorous, controlled conditions, as well as out in "the field" under natural conditions. The result has been proof that our memory of events, faces, persons, colors, objects, and the like is reconstructive and *de*constructive, making our testimony about that memory tremendously unreliable, far more unreliable than most people would naturally suppose.

Gardner liked to shake up his readers' prejudices by having Perry Mason point out that, while eye-witness testimony is treacherous, circumstantial evidence, which most people view as shaky, is actually the best kind of courtroom evidence:

> "In the mind of the average man, circumstantial evidence most frequently results in a miscarriage of justice. Actually, circumstantial evidence is the best evidence we have. It is only our interpretation of circumstantial evidence which makes for miscarriages of justice. The most deadly, dangerous evidence, the one which has resulted so many, many times in miscarriages of justice, is personal identification evidence." (*The Case of the Foot-Loose Doll*)

Now here's the final kicker for you to think about: Everyone knows that a jury's primary job is to weigh all the evidence presented at trial. However, isn't it true that any piece of evidence ultimately *depends upon* eyewitness testimony? If a document is produced in evidence, then someone has to look at the document and read what it says—a matter of using their eyes. And the document itself must have been written by someone, who presumably depended on the evidence of their senses—most often their eyes. A coroner's report, for example, would be issued by a doctor who used his or her eyes to examine the deceased's body. Even a photograph of someone actually committing a crime relies on someone to look at the photograph and interpret what it shows. And all of those folks exonerated through DNA testing had some DNA expert—perhaps a lab technician or other scientist—who testified in court that they saw the test results or saw that the pair of pants that had the DNA was found at the crime scene.

So, on one hand there's all of this research showing how unreliable witness testimony is, making it dubious and suspect for courtroom proceedings, especially those criminal trials where the standard of proof is "beyond a reasonable doubt" (the prosecution must prove that the defendant is guilty of the crime charged to the extent that no reasonable person could have a reasonable doubt that the defendant is guilty). But, on the other hand much of the evidence presented in court still ultimately depends on eyewitnesses inspecting crime scenes, examining dead bodies, logging murder weapons, scanning documents, and other perception- and memory-related activities, and we can assume these eyewitnesses suffer from the same kinds of faulty perception and memory problems that the folks who sit on the stand and claim, "Yes, that's him. He's the one who did it" in the courtroom.

The whole situation is a paradox. Let's see Mr. Mason try and defend this one!

# 6
# The Facts Don't Speak for Themselves

KATHRYN MUYSKENS

Perry Mason's clients are always innocent, at least as they are presented through the course of the classic *Perry Mason* television series (1957–1966). Yet, the police are able to find enough evidence to suspect them of murder, and even to bring them to trial. On the other hand, Mason is always able to uncover evidence of his client's innocence, which is almost always evidence that the crime was committed by someone else. Why is this happening?

Why are Lieutenant Tragg and Mason finding facts and interpreting the evidence so differently? Why do the real culprits so often escape the initial notice of the police? Does this discrepancy reflect a degree of incompetence by the police in the Perry Mason universe? Or are they justified in believing Mason's clients are guilty?

If no, then the police must be incompetent or indeed malicious for bringing Mason's clients to trial. If yes, then that may lead us to a more disturbing puzzle. Why should good evidence so often point to the wrong person? Is there something wrong with what counts as evidence in the *Perry Mason* world?

The philosopher David Hume, writing in his *Treatise of Human Nature*, distinguished between two different kinds of knowledge. First, there was the kind of knowledge we can gain from the "mere operation of thought." These are necessary truths that describe relationships between ideas—for example: a triangle has three sides. It's impossible to imagine a triangle that does not fit this description, because the three sides are what make it a triangle. We don't need to test or observe any actual triangles in the world to know this.

But the other kind of knowledge, which Hume called "matters of fact," did not work this way. Matters of fact are different from necessary truths because they describe events in the world which we can imagine being otherwise. For example, we know that Obama was elected to two terms as president, but there is nothing about the nature of Obama or the presidency that makes this *necessarily* the case. In each election, it was possible that Obama could have lost to his opponent, but it is just the matter of fact that he did not.

The way that we know matters of fact is very different from the way we know about the properties of a triangle. We learn about our world through observation, but since we cannot observe everything, we make inferences from things we have observed. Essentially, we use our past experience and project it onto the future. This kind of thinking is called inductive reasoning. Inductive reasoning looks like this:

>PREMISE: All dogs I have met in the past have been friendly.

>CONCLUSION: All dogs I will meet in the future will also be friendly.

This example highlights the usefulness and potential dangers of using inductive reasoning. The dogs I meet in the future might continue to be friendly, but if I rely too heavily on this prediction I might be unprepared for the eventual unfriendly dog and might get bitten as a result. It is possible my encounters with dogs will never directly contradict this belief of mine, and yet—I can hardly say I *know* that all dogs are friendly.

Let's look at another hypothetical example. Imagine you are a paleontologist and you find an ancient species of unknown animal preserved in the permafrost. Let's call it Species X. You take it to your lab and study it. When you study it, you see that its skin is covered in a woolly coat of fur, and you also discover that all four of its legs are broken.

## The Facts Don't Speak for Themselves

There are several conclusions about the new species you could make from these findings. You can conclude that all other members of Species X were covered in woolly fur. You could also conclude that all of the other members of Species X had four broken legs. Both are conclusions you can arrive at through induction, and since this is the only example of Species X in existence, you have equal evidence (numerically speaking) for each conclusion. Yet, we tend to think in this example that the first conclusion is more likely to be true than the second. But why? Any justification we give for this is likely to be inductive itself, and therein lies the problem.

There is no support for inductive reasoning that is not itself inductive. Just as defining a word in the dictionary by using the word itself fails to explain what it means, the same is true for relying on inductive reasoning. Even though it often works in our favor and gives us the kind of predictions we rely upon in life, we ought to be skeptical and prepared for the times when it does not produce a good conclusion.

## Testing Rival Theories

What counts as proof in a courtroom might be very different than what would satisfy philosophers. In the legal system, Mason only really needs to produce *reasonable doubt* that his client did not commit the crime in order for the jury to acquit. Despite creating reasonable doubt being all that is required of him legally, Mason himself, much like a philosopher, does not seem to want to stop there. He presses further to the point where there is not only reasonable doubt about his client's innocence, but reveals something which the audience, even Burger and Tragg, take to be *proof* that they are innocent—and proof that someone else is guilty!

Philosophers have a name for this type of certainty—*justified true belief*. This is the philosopher's recipe for knowledge. In order to know something, the subject must have a belief, the belief must be true, and the subject must have some justification for believing it to be true. What does it mean for a belief to be justified? Basically, it comes down to evidence. Evidence could be based on experience, observation, inference, or experimentation. But evidence can be tricky. Sometimes evidence can be misleading, and it's difficult to sift out what evidence may be relevant in any given case.

So, how does this apply in the *Perry Mason* world? The typical *Perry Mason* case begins with someone (often an unlikable someone) being murdered. No one will be there to see what happens first-hand except for the killer. Plenty of people will be plausible suspects, but Lieutenant Tragg and Hamilton Burger will quickly settle on one person as their prime suspect. This person either already is, or will quickly become, Mason's client. Mason will gather evidence in their defense and through the course of the case he will not only prove his client's innocence, but will also induce a confession from the real culprit.

But why (without inferring from past *Perry Mason* episodes) should we believe that Mason's explanation of the crime is better than Tragg's and Burger's? Why and how did they come to different conclusions in the first place? To find the answer we must first establish what justifications Mason, Tragg, and Burger have for their beliefs, and also how they each acquired that knowledge so that we can determine which explanation is more likely to be correct.

In "The Case of the Shapely Shadow," some of the differences in Mason's approach compared to Tragg's and Burger's can be readily seen. Janice Wainwright comes into Mason's office because she's concerned that her boss Mr. Theilman is being blackmailed. She has found a note that her boss received that was constructed from newspaper cut outs, like a classic ransom note. It read, "Get money. Instructions on telephone. Failure will be fatal." Next thing she knows, Theilman has asked her to take a briefcase to a locker with a note labeled "A.B. Vidal, General Delivery."

As *Perry Mason* episodes so often play out, her boss is eventually found dead and she is the unwitting suspect! Once the case finally makes it to the courtroom, Hamilton Burger lays out his case.

The prosecution's version of the story is that Janice was blackmailing Theilman. They infer that it was she who made the threatening note from newspaper clippings, and she went to pick up the blackmail money herself. She met Theilman in the model home and shot him, and then set up the meeting with Theilman's first wife in Las Vegas to cover her tracks.

### The Facts Don't Speak for Themselves

As evidence for their theory of the crime, Burger presents testimony from:

1. A tire-track expert who testifies that the tracks match Janice's car.
2. A medical examiner who testifies that the time of death was between midnight and 5:00 A.M. based on the lividity.
3. A co-worker at Janice's office who testifies that he had seen Theilman kiss her, and that she was always following him around like "a slave."
4. Cole B. Troy, who testifies that after his meeting with Theilman he saw a shapely female figure follow Theilman as he left.
5. Theilman's first wife, who testifies that she was surprised to see Janice was the one waiting for her.
6. A taxi driver who claims to have received bills from Janice. The bills do indeed match the serial numbers of the blackmail money.
7. Lieutenant Tragg, who testifies that the newspaper clippings come from two particular newspapers, *The Chronicle* and *The Bullet*, which Janice was seen purchasing.

## Believing His Client

Mason does his best to undermine each point in Burger's case, and is successful in some, but not others. He is able to make the medical examiner's time of death seem less reliable, by pointing out an article that the man himself had written in the past that makes his certainty about the time of death seem suspect. And Mason also makes Mr. Troy's testimony seem shaky since he can't seem to get it straight where he was looking when he saw this "shapely shadow." But the rest of the evidence Burger has compiled seems quite solid... and damning for Mason's client.

During a break in the trial Mason reviews the case with Janice. She tells him she doesn't want to go on the stand, but also insists that she didn't commit the crime. She was sincerely following orders from Theilman the whole time. The day of his death he had told her to stay out of sight, so she went to a beauty parlor for the day and left her car in the lot. Mason takes note of this and also the times that the lot would have been locked so he can know if and when someone else would have been able to use her car.

Back in court, Mason then re-interviews the first Mrs. Theilman and asks her if she had ever had dealings with someone called A.B. Vidal. She says yes, a man called her using that name and pressed her to sell her stock to him. She refused but agreed to discuss it if Theilman would meet her in Las Vegas in person. She says Vidal paid for the trip to Las Vegas. He had sent her money—all twenty-dollar bills, just like the blackmail money.

Once Mason has finished questioning her, she goes back to her seat and Burger makes a very telling comment as she passes him, "You never told me you knew anyone named Vidal." "You never asked," she replies.

Then it comes time for the closing arguments. In his final speech to the jury, Mason gives his alternate explanation of the crime. He presents no new facts into evidence, but instead of painting Janice at the center of a blackmail plot, Mason places Theilman himself. Theilman was trying to retain control of his company. His only hope in this endeavor was to get the last shares of stock from his former wife. He approached her under an assumed name, A.B. Vidal. A name which legally belonged to his current wife, so any stock signed over to that name would still be accessible to him. Mason argues that it was Theilman himself who constructed the blackmail note from newspaper clippings, and that he made sure that both Janice and his wife saw them to give his secret deal a believable cover. It was he, not Janice, who later removed all the money from that locker. Theilman, Mason argues, was even intending to keep the meeting with his former wife to get those last stock shares. He used the "blackmail" money to pay for his ex-wife's trip to Las Vegas, and one of those bills wound up with the taxi driver.

Mason stokes doubt about the time of death yet again, and points out that while Janice was at the beauty parlor, anyone could have had access to her car. All they would have needed to do to frame her for Theilman's murder is to wet the ground enough to make sure her car would leave some tracks, making it appear that she had been there close to the time it rained and to the time for which she had no alibi. Mason presents the photo of the model home, pointing out that there is a hose readily available for just such a task. His account neatly fits each piece of evidence, but with a different explanation.

Naturally, Burger declares this to be "pure poppycock!" Burger reiterates his theory of the crime, calling Janice a "shrewd scheming woman. She seduced her employer, she stole from him, and finally murdered him." Burger goes on to say that the location of the murder is an abandoned real estate development—the water hasn't been running for years! Mason quickly accuses Burger of "stating facts not in evidence." So, the court is manipulated into producing one more witness to establish whether in fact there was any water on the property. The evidence until now was not part of either side's theory of the case, but once the records are produced they resolve the mystery once and for all.

The water had indeed not been running on the property for years. But it was turned on the day of the murder—and the records show who turned it on: Cole B. Troy. Right on cue, as the evidence is revealed, Troy sighs and says, "I . . . I did it . . . I killed him." Case closed.

In "The Case of the Shapely Shadow," it seems that Tragg and Burger do have reasons to believe Janice is guilty. Their reasons even seem to be good ones. She really does appear to be guilty! Mason is just privy to a bit more information than them—because he has access to Janice, and he trusts her account. Because he trusts her, he pushes just a bit further than the prosecution to reveal that last piece of evidence that proves his explanation is the correct one. Until that point, Mason and Burger have different interpretations of the evidence, but there doesn't seem to be anything fishy going on from the prosecution's side. Both versions are reasonable explanations. Only one is true. But Burger and Tragg aren't making any serious or reckless errors in their thinking.

## The Vanishing Body

In other cases, however, Tragg and Burger's explanations differ from Mason's in ways that seem less forgivable. Take, for example "The Case of the Runaway Corpse."

Ed Davenport has not been well. He suspects his ill health is not due to natural causes. He has just had a lab technician test the contents of some sandwiches his wife had made for him. The technician reveals that they are loaded with arsenic. Someone is trying to poison Mr. Davenport! Mr. Davenport already has someone in mind as the culprit—his own wife, Myrna. He promptly goes home and confronts her about his suspicions in front of her cousin, Louise. He even accuses Myrna of having previously poisoned her own uncle in the same manner. Before leaving to go on a business trip, he informs her that he has left a letter with his real estate office to be released to the authorities if he should die. The letter accuses her of his murder.

Apparently believing that this letter will protect him from further poisoning, he then takes his bags (including some chocolates) that Myrna has packed and leaves. Louise eventually convinces Myrna that she should see a lawyer, just in case anything happens to her husband and someone really does accuse her of murder. The lawyer, of course, is Perry Mason.

Almost as soon as Mason is hired, Louise gets a call that Ed is gravely sick. She and Myrna make the trip down to check on him. Myrna sees Ed lying in bed, apparently very ill, but when he sees her, he becomes frightened and once again accuses her of poisoning him.

Meanwhile, Mason and Della sneak into Mr. Davenport's office and find the letter in which he accuses his wife of his murder. They steam it open to get a look at what it says inside (and to enable them to reseal it later with no one the wiser). Mason tells Della he noticed a large withdrawal of money was made from Mr. Davenport's account that very day. Once the letter is opened, they discover it to be blank! "Invisible ink?" Della wonders aloud. They hold it over a heat source to check—but no writing appears.

Soon after, the doctor declares Ed dead. Tragg arrives to begin investigating. The doctor tells Tragg that his patient accused his wife of poisoning him. Myrna tells Tragg that her husband had a heart attack. But when they go in to check on the body, it has vanished!

The police, as well as Hamilton Burger, assume that Mr. Davenport has been murdered, and go to find the letter he left. They too discover it to be blank, but assume that Mason has tampered with it on Myrna's behalf.

Even without the body, and without the letter spelling out an accusation, Tragg soon comes to arrest Myrna—not for her husband's murder (yet) but for her uncle's! In that very moment, her cousin Louise turns on her too. She accuses Myrna of both murders in front of Tragg in an angry outburst. It doesn't take too long before Mr. Davenport's body reappears, this time in a ditch some ways away. Myrna is soon on trial for both murders.

At trial, Burger presents a medical examiner once again, who testifies that Mr. Davenport died of arsenic poisoning. The witness also testifies that the arsenic was consumed within an hour of Mr. Davenport's death. He goes on to say that he tested the candies and found that they contained arsenic.

When Mason cross-examines, however, he adds that though the candies contained arsenic it is not his opinion that they were the cause of Mr. Davenport's death. Mr. Davenport had also recently eaten a meal of bacon and eggs and had some alcohol, and, in his expert opinion, it was in this meal that the arsenic was ingested.

Burger then calls the doctor who was tending to Mr. Davenport on his deathbed. The doctor testifies that when Mr. Davenport died, he immediately pumped his stomach and that is why none of the candies were found in his system later. Burger seems to miss the rather glaring fact that the previous witness just testified that Mr. Davenport's body was found with a meal of bacon and eggs inside—but Mason picks up on this quickly and uses it to contest the time of death the prosecution is arguing.

Mason presses the doctor about his testimony and asks him whether Mr. Davenport requested him to help him fake his death. The doctor responds by saying that "the communication between a doctor and his patient is privileged!"

## Jumping to the Wrong Conclusion

Mason then asks the doctor about his medical degree and gets him to admit that it is from a now non-existent and unaccredited school. Then, once again, Mason raises the accusation that the doctor was conspiring with Mr. Davenport to fake his own death and to frame his wife. The doctor invokes the Fifth Amendment.

Mason next calls Mr. Beckmeyer, Mr. Davenport's private investigator. Mason asks him if he helped Mr. Davenport plan to set up his wife and fake his own death. Beckmeyer essentially admits to helping Mr. Davenport set up bank accounts under false names to hide money away from Myrna, and to helping him set up the evidence to frame her.

Mason goes one step further and accuses Beckmeyer of giving Mr. Davenport the poisoned bacon and eggs. Under the pressure of Mason's accusations, Beckmeyer cracks. He admits, "Well, the chump was asking for it . . . He was going to disappear and leave his wife holding the bag. Everyone would wonder what happened to the body. It was such a great plan, I figured with a little help from me, it would be perfect." Beckmeyer's confession closes the case.

Just as in "The Case of the Shapely Shadow," Mason has more information than Tragg and Burger simply because he has (and believes) his client's account. Yet, there's something more at work in this case. Tragg and Burger settle on their suspect before Mr. Davenport is even dead. That's too fast for their actions to make sense. True, they have reason to believe Myrna is guilty—her husband and later her cousin both accuse her of being a serial poisoner! However, it only takes a little consideration to realize that this information isn't very reliable. How Burger and Tragg missed the obvious contradictions in their own witnesses' testimony is astounding! And their failure to investigate other options or check their sources demonstrates a complete disregard for the truth, especially in the bizarre case of a runaway corpse! It's as if they're not even trying!

So, what is it that makes Mason so good at finding the truth and Burger and Tragg so bad at it? Well, the short answer seems to be that Mason cares to look. Part of the difference between Mason and the prosecution is that Burger "fails to see the relevance of this line of inquiry" as he so often declares in court. More than that, Tragg and Burger are just plain lazy. They form a belief (that Myrna is guilty) on flimsy justification (her husband's accusation) and ignore all evidence to the contrary. They stop asking questions far too early.

### The Facts Don't Speak for Themselves

Burger and Tragg seem more interested in closing a case quickly, using the most obvious and convenient suspect, than they are in actually getting to the bottom of the puzzle. Unlike them, Mason is tireless and energetic in his investigations. He withholds judgment until the evidence is in and he actively searches for evidence that would support or contradict other possible explanations of a crime. Mason digs deeper into justified belief. He asks his client for her honest account, then he checks the evidence that could back her up or prove she is lying, then and only then does he take her word for it. He thoroughly investigates the other suspects and gathers evidence with the help of Paul Drake and Della Street. In the end, he winds up with much more justification for his beliefs than Tragg and Burger have for theirs. This is how investigation is supposed to work. And this is why Mason's explanations of the evidence are reliable and true.

# 7
# Beyond a Reasonable Doubt

DOUGLAS JORDAN

> There was one murder per week in this community, so you'd think that, under the law of averages, the law-enforcement authorities, led by District Attorney Hamilton Burger, would at least occasionally arrest a guilty person. But they *never* did. They *always* arrested an innocent person, and that person *always* hired Perry Mason, who *always* won the case.
>
> —DAVE BARRY, *Dave Barry Turns 50*

> Therefore, you have no *choice* but to find him *not guilty*.
>
> —PERRY MASON

Perry Mason is an extraordinary defense attorney. He seems to always show that his client is innocent. This could be attributed to any number of reasons, but three come to mind.

> The first is that Perry Mason always represents a small subset of clients within the American legal system who happen to be falsely accused and actually innocent.
>
> The second is that Perry Mason possesses an incredible legal prowess that deftly manages to defeat any adversary who could hope to prove one of his clients guilty.
>
> The third reason is that the laws of logic are on the side of Perry Mason and all other American defense attorneys.

## Douglas Jordan

Well, Perry Mason does seem to have a way of choosing seemingly guilty clients who turn out to be innocent, and he does have a legendary legal prowess. However, the strongest weapon in Perry Mason's arsenal in the defense of his client's innocence is the immutable and powerful laws of logic. The strongest of these laws in support of Perry is the law of induction, and its close ally, the problem of induction. These two principles of thinking, in conjunction with the rules of the American legal system and deductive logic all but guarantee Perry Mason a win in court.

Under American law, in a criminal case, the defendant cannot be found guilty unless the judge in a bench trial or jury in a jury trial agrees that he is guilty beyond a reasonable doubt. A jury's decision to find guilty and convict must be unanimous. In the Perry Mason books, television show, and made for TV movies, the trial is almost always in front of a jury. This jury, as in all others, is a twelve-person sampling of the county in which the crime is brought to trial. In *Perry Mason*, this occurs in Los Angeles County in California.

The judge or jury arrives at its decision as the result of a trial. During the trial, both the defendant and prosecutor get a chance to produce evidence. The defendant is trying to show that he is innocent, while the state is trying to show his guilt. Perry Mason is the defense attorney, representing the client. His opponent, representing the state of California is the district attorney, Hamilton Burger.

Evidence takes one of two forms, testimony or physical evidence. Testimony is given by the witness in response to either the defendant's or state's questions. Physical evidence is tangible pieces of evidence that people may touch and examine. Testimonial evidence is elicited by attorneys such as Mason or Burger during court.

Consider Perry's cross examination in *The Case of the Howling Dog* (1934). Here, Perry presents testimonial evidence through the cab driver when his eyewitness identification is discredited as a case of mistaken identity. In the same case, Perry introduces physical evidence of a handwritten note and telegram in order to prove the identities of three separate women. This ultimately allows him to win his case. Very rarely in a criminal case does the state have clear evidence that the defendant is guilty. Criminals are rarely kind enough to allow themselves to be caught on camera committing the crime, followed by giving a full confession to all elements of the offense. This requires that the elements of the crime be proven in court.

No amount of probabilities and possibilities can lead to a certainty. 'Maybe he did', 'I think I saw him', and 'It might be him' cannot become a guilty verdict. There is a transition that must be made from inductive logic and argument to deductive logic and argument. Argument is built on logic and premises. Logic is the mathematical structure of the argument. Premises are the claims that are advanced in the argument. This is known as the problem of induction, first formulated by Greek philosophers, and refined by David Hume (1711–1776) and Karl Popper (1902–1994). As a result of the problem of induction, no amount of evidence can be presented to prove a person guilty. This results in Perry Mason allowing his client to walk free.

## Deductive Logic

Deductive logic entails that the conclusion of an argument can be absolutely guaranteed by the premises given. The strength of a deductive argument is that when the premises are sound and the logic is valid, then the conclusion is guaranteed to be true.

Look at the following argument:

1. If Perry Mason wins his case, then he will have another client.
2. Perry Mason wins his case.
3. Therefore, Perry Mason will have another client.

Soundness of an argument is when all claims (premises) of an argument are true. If one of the statements in the argument is not true, then the truth of the conclusion cannot be relied upon. But if both statements are true, the conclusion must be true. In the above argument, we can assume that both statements 1. and 2. are true. If one or both the statements were false, then the argument would not guarantee the truth of the conclusion. The following example is an argument with valid structure, though the conclusion is not true.

1. Della Street is the secretary for Perry Mason.
2. If Della Street is the secretary for Perry Mason, then Hamilton Burger will win his case.
3. Therefore, Hamilton Burger will win his case.

In the above argument, the second claim is false. There is no relation between Della being Perry's secretary and Hamilton winning a case. While the structure of the argument is valid, the claims themselves are not all true, rendering the conclusion unreliable.

Validity of an argument is when the mathematical structure of the argument, also known as the logic of the argument, is correct. Sound and true premises in the absence of a valid argument will be unable to guarantee or even suggest the truth of the conclusion. In the above argument, the structure used is modus ponens, one of eight basic argument structures. Below is an example of an invalid argument structure.

1. Perry Mason is a lawyer.
2. Perry Mason has detective skills.
3. Therefore, Erle Stanley Gardner wrote the original Perry Mason books.

While all of the statements are true, there is no causation or link between the statements and the conclusion. This is an invalid argument: although the conclusion happens to be true, it does not follow from the premises.

## Inductive Logic

In deductive logic, the conclusion follows from the premises with certainty. In inductive logic, there is no guaranteed truth to the conclusion, but there is strong evidence and support. Consider the following argument:

1. In all of the cases so far, Perry Mason either wins his case, or the state loses via a mistrial.
2. Therefore, it is likely that Perry Mason will win his next case.

An inductive argument does not guarantee the truth of its conclusion by the truth of its premises. The premises of an inductive argument can be true, and the argument can be valid, but the conclusion is not always true. In the case above, the conclusion is based on what we have seen and have good reason to believe.

## The Problem of Induction

The problem of induction underlies the issue of proof in any criminal court. Simply, there is no amount of circumstantial evidence that can be used to conclusively prove any legal element of a crime.

Inductive reasoning holds that we should believe a conclusion based on the strength of its claims. When we look at the win record of Perry Mason, we have good reason to think that he will win his next case. However, good reason to think something is true is not the same standard as beyond a reasonable doubt.

Greek philosopher Sextus Empiricus (160–210) was one of the first to consider the issue posed by the problem of induction. His name later goes on to form the basis of the empiricist school of thought, which holds that concrete proof and empirical evidence is needed. While Sextus did not frame his objection as the problem of induction, he demonstrates this problem through regression arguments, which is a form of skepticism. The regression argument shows that to have knowledge about something, there is a requirement that justification exists. However, the justification is also a piece of knowledge, which would require additional justification. The regression argument essentially becomes a call for justifications of justifications upon justifications. Regression arguments such as Sextus makes are precisely why Perry Mason should not lose.

David Hume was the first modern philosopher to seriously consider the implications and possible solutions to the problem of induction. Hume does not call the problem of induction by this name. Hume questions how a person can form an opinion about an unseen event, and what level of justification arises from such reasoning. This is precisely what is at stake when we discuss Perry Mason. Perry has an advantage over the state when it comes to proving his case.

Perry Mason can rely on the problem of induction to show the weakness in Hamilton Burger's case. Burger has the burden of proof. This means that Burger must prove beyond a reasonable doubt that Perry's client committed whichever crime they are being charged with. In the TV movie *Perry Mason Returns* (1985), when Della is accused of murder, the prosecutor must prove that Della committed murder beyond a reasonable doubt. Meanwhile, Perry gets to rely on the problem of induction to show that Della is innocent of the crimes she is accused of.

Della, like all other Americans, enjoy the protection of a jury trial. In a criminal case, the defendant cannot be convicted unless the judge in a bench trial or jury in a jury trial agrees that the defendant is guilty beyond a reasonable doubt. The decision to find guilty and convict must be unanimous. No one member may feel that there is a chance that the defendant is innocent.

Perry Mason's talents, in addition to the laws of logic, and the problem of induction, will ensure that in the days to come, our hero will never lose a case.

# 8
# Taking Evidence Personally

ANTHONY BECKER AND CHARLES TALIAFERRO

"Crime is personal. Evidence of crime is impersonal," Perry Mason tells his faithful, intrepid secretary. Della Street is asking her Chief (as she sometimes calls him) about his methods. How does Perry decide whom to defend and why? Would he defend someone whom he thought was guilty? Mason replies to Della:

> "I never take a case unless I'm convinced my client was incapable of committing the crime charged. Once I've reached that conclusion, I figure there must be some discrepancies between the evidence and the conclusions the police have drawn from that evidence. I set out to find them." (*The Case of the Perjured Parrot*, p. 3)

But how does that work?

## Measuring Evidence

One of the most famous devices used to weigh evidence is called Bayes's Theorem, named for Reverend Thomas Bayes (1701–1761), who developed the foundations of the theorem. Though worked out in the eighteenth century, the theorem is very much in use today in logic, probability, and statistical estimation. The application of Bayes's Theorem to the analysis of both probabilistic events and data involves the following fundamental relationship:

$$P(G|E) = \frac{P(G|E) \cdot P(G)}{P(E)}$$

In this formula, the function $P(\cdot)$ represents the probability of some state of the world or set of facts. For example, let $G$ represent the guilt of Mason's client and let $E$ represent the evidence (a set of facts) available to the reader or viewer. Then,

$P(G)$ = the probability of Mason's client's guilt, and

$P(E)$ = the probability of the evidence

The vertical bar between two states or sets denotes that the first is conditional upon the second being true or observed. This is a conditional probability.

$P(G|E)$ = the probability of $G$ given $E$ is true
= the probability the client is guilty given the evidence

While $P(G|E)$ and $P(E|G)$ are easily confused, they are rarely equal and the value of one is often quite different from the value of the other. Bayes's Theorem is used to transform one conditional probability into the other, for instance, to go from $P(E|G)$ to $P(G|E)$.

First we must understand that these two conditional probabilities can often differ considerably. Consider "The Case of the Restless Redhead." Evelyn Bagby finds a gun in her apartment that is a murder weapon. Let $G$ = {Evelyn is guilty} and $E$ = {Evelyn is found with the murder weapon}. Then the notation $P(E|G)$ means "the probability that Evelyn is found with the murder weapon given that (or if) she is guilty." The notation $P(G|E)$ means "the probability that Evelyn is guilty given that (if) she is found with the murder weapon." In the first case, if she were guilty (the condition), there would be a good chance for the murder weapon to be found in her possession. In the second case, even though the gun is found in her possession (the condition), we know that there is no chance she is guilty.

The value of Bayes's Theorem is that it gives us a way of getting from $P(E|G)$ to $P(G|E)$. In the situations of the

## Taking Evidence Personally

Mason stories, as in Bayesian analysis, we can treat $P(E)$ as constant. The set of evidence is what it is. (Though Mason may, at times, alter the evidence as we discuss below.) That set of evidence had some fixed probability of occurring. Then, the probability the client is guilty given (conditional upon) the set of facts, $P(G\mid E)$, is proportional to the product of $P(E\mid G)$ and $P(G)$. This is written mathematically as:

$$P(G\mid E) \propto P(E\mid G) \cdot P(G)$$

Rather than think of $P(G)$ as a single value, we can think of it as a function that gives probabilities for all the possible values of $G$. This is known as the *prior distribution*. The probability of the evidence given that the client is guilty, $P(E\mid G)$, we will call the *likelihood function*. Finally, the probability the client is guilty given the facts is the *posterior distribution*, and is proportional to the likelihood multiplied by the prior distribution.

## Mason's Reasoning Confronted with the Police's Reasoning

Here's a simple numerical example. First, in a simple case, the client is either guilty or not. That is, $G = \{\text{guilty, innocent}\} = \{1, 0\}$. Then our prior distribution, $P(G)$, needs to assign values (probabilities) for the two possible values of $G$. Suppose that we believe there is a fifty-fifty chance the client is guilty.

Next, we need a likelihood function, $P(E\mid G)$. This function will assess the likelihood (probability) of us having seen the set of evidence for all the possible values of $G$. Let's say that $P(E\mid G=1) = 0.8$ and $P(E\mid G=0) = 0.2$. This means that there is an eighty percent chance of seeing the set of facts if the client is guilty ($G = 1$) and a twenty percent chance of seeing that set of facts if the client is innocent ($G = 0$).

Bayes's Theorem says then that the probability of guilt given the facts is

$$P(G=1\mid E) \propto P(E\mid G=1) \cdot P(G=1) = 0.8 \cdot 0.6 = 0.4 = 40\%$$

and the probability of innocence given the facts is

$P(G = 0 \mid E) \propto P(E \mid G = 0) \cdot P(G = 0) = 0.2 \cdot 0.5 = 0.1 = 10\%$

To make this a true posterior distribution, we need the two values to total one hundred percent which we accomplish by doubling each of them. (This is equivalent to saying that $P(E) = 1/2$.) Our posterior distribution becomes

$P(G = 1 \mid E) = 40\% \times 2 = 80\%$

$P(G = 0 \mid E) = 10\% \times 2 = 20\%$

Which means that our posterior belief is that there is an 80% chance the client is guilty. Put another way, the client is four times more likely to be guilty than innocent.

There are two key characteristics of the Mason story lines where Bayes's Theorem is relevant. First, Mason only takes a case if he believes his client is innocent and the authorities—the police and prosecutor—only pursue a case where they believe the client is guilty. Mason and the authorities have substantially different prior distributions or $P(G)$.

Second, the authorities often seem to commit a common mistake of not recognizing the difference between $P(E \mid G)$ and $P(G \mid E)$. The prosecutorial failure is to focus on $P(E \mid G)$, the probability of the evidence given the guilt of the defendant. What Mason wants the judge or jury to do is focus on $P(G \mid E)$, the probability of guilt given the evidence.

From Mason's perspective, only taking the cases of innocent clients means that his prior distribution is $P(G = 1) = 0 = 0\%$ and $P(G = 1) = 1 = 100\%$. Using the same likelihoods as before, for Mason, the posterior probability of guilt given the facts is proportionate to:

$P(G = 1 \mid E) \propto P(E \mid G = 1) \cdot P(G = 1) = 0.8 \cdot 0 = 0\%$

and the posterior probability of innocence given the facts is proportionate to:

$P(G = 0 \mid E) \propto P(E \mid G = 0) \cdot P(G = 0) = 0.2 \cdot 1 = 20\%$

Multiplying by five gives the proportional values that add to 100%: $P(G = 1 \mid E) = 0\%$ and $P(G = 0 \mid E) = 100\%$. His client is certainly innocent.

## Taking Evidence Personally

No matter how damning the evidence, Mason's posterior distribution tells him that it is infinitely more likely that the client is innocent than guilty. Even if we were to suppose that the chance of seeing the set of evidence given an innocent client is only 1% (or ), then

$$P(G = 1 | E) \propto P(E | G = 1) \cdot P(G = 1) = 0.99 \cdot 0 = 0\%$$
$$P(G = 0 | E) \propto P(E | G = 0) \cdot P(G = 0) = 0.01 \cdot 1 = 1\%$$

Multiplying both by 100 gives us and . Mason, as a Bayesian, still concludes that his client is certainly innocent.

The police and prosecutor may believe there is some doubt of the client's guilt but they are clearly sure it is more likely than not that Mason's client is guilty. Let's say that the authorities' prior distribution is

$$P(G = 0) = 20\% \text{ and } P(G = 1) = 80\%$$

Given this prior, even if the set of evidence were somewhat less likely to have occurred with a guilty client as with an innocent one, the authorities, if they too are Bayesians, will have a posterior distribution that points towards guilt.

With

$$P(E | G) = 0) = 60\% \text{ and } P(E | G) = 1) = 40\%$$

then

$$P(G = 1 | E) \propto P(E | G = 1) \cdot P(G = 1) = 0.4 \cdot 0.8 = 32\%$$
$$P(G = 0 | E) \propto P(E | G = 0) \cdot P(G = 0) = 0.6 \cdot 0.2 = 12\%$$

To make this a proper posterior distribution, divide both values by 44%:

$$P(G = 1 | E) = 32\% \left(\frac{1}{44\%}\right) = 72.7\%$$
$$P(G = 0 | E) = 12\% \left(\frac{1}{44\%}\right) = 27.3\%$$

This second example illustrates the second failure: of not recognizing the difference between $P(E\mid G)$ and $P(G\mid E)$. With a chance of guilt given the evidence that is less than 50%, a prior which strongly favors guilt, overwhelms the likelihood and causes the posterior distribution to favor guilt. Hamilton Burger and the police fall into this trap each time. Their prior distribution creates a posterior distribution that confirms what they would like to be true of the likelihood.

In Bayesian analysis of data, great care is taken in the formation of priors so that an extreme prior does not restrict the posterior distribution unrealistically. In the Mason stories, we can predict the extreme priors of the police—Lieutenant Tragg, for example—by their demeanors alone. When the likelihood is greater for the evidence at hand given a guilty client than given innocence, multiplication by a prior strongly in favor of guilt, leads inexorably to a posterior prior that also favors guilt. The agreement in direction between $P(G\mid E)$ and $P(E\mid G)$ leads some to confuse the two as equivalent.

We arrive then at the issue of Mason's evidence tampering. In "The Case of the Nervous Accomplice" he destroys a cab receipt and then has his client generate another, nearly identical receipt; he fires two bullets at a crime scene in "The Case of the Restless Redhead"; and he substitutes a bird in "The Case of the Perjured Parrot." In all three cases, the "evidence" Mason has fabricated is entered as exhibits in the proceedings.

From a Bayesian perspective, Mason has augmented the set of evidence so as to change the likelihood. Let the augmented set of evidence be $E'$. Mason constructs the additional evidence so that

$$P(E'\mid G) < P(E\mid G)$$

Regardless of the prior, a lower likelihood will reduce the posterior probability. Holding $P(G)$ constant,

$$\{P(E'\mid G) < P(E\mid G)\} \Rightarrow \{P(G\mid E') < P(G\mid E)\}$$

(The symbol $\Rightarrow$ is read as "implies.") Thus, Mason's fabrication of evidence is designed to overcome the prosecutorial prior favoring the guilt of his client. Given the augmented set of evidence, the prosecutor's case routinely begins to unravel giving Mason the opening to elicit the confession of the true perpetrator.

The fabricated evidence is occasionally intended to elicit a reaction from a character. Returning, for example, to "The Case of the Nervous Accomplice," Mason's introduction of the shooting stand causes the murderer to reveal himself (off camera) and unhinges the accomplice sufficiently so that she reveals the perpetrator in open court.

This manipulation of the evidence seems astonishing in terms of legal ethics, but Mr. Mason seems to be led to do so by his independent confidence in (and his estimation of the prior probability of) his client's innocence to shift the evidential landscape, exposing points where incriminating evidence is either innocuous or points to the guilt of another party. We now seek to make explicit this guiding principle employed by Mason which we refer to as 'Taking evidence personally.'

## Personal Evidence Makes All the Difference

In a reflective moment before the main plot of *The Case of the Perjured Parrot* gets underway, Della Street quizzes her Boss's method. She is responding to Perry Mason's explanation about why he defends the clients he does in terms of sizing up evidence. Della "laughed. 'You sound as though you were more of a detective than a lawyer.'" Mason replies:

> "No... they are two different professions. A detective gathers evidence. He becomes skilled in knowing what to look for, where to find it, and how to get it. A lawyer interprets the evidence after it's collected." (*The Case of the Perjured Parrot*, p. 3)

As we know, Mason does some detective work (or has Paul Drake do so on his behalf) and Mason is not above creating evidence. But Mason's interpretation of the evidence is guided by his independent conviction about his client as a person: "I never take a case unless I'm convinced my client was incapable of committing the crime charged. Once I've reached that conclusion, I figure there must be some discrepancy between the evidence and the conclusions the police have drawn from that evidence. I set out to find them" (p. 3). Mason's method at this stage, prior to assigning probability factors to evidence involves a kind of taking evidence personally.

There is some danger that taking evidence personally can result in the stubbornness that Mason complains about with the police.

> Once a man forms an opinion, he starts interpreting facts in light of that belief. He ceases to be an impartial judge of facts. That's what's happened to Raymond Sprague. He's come to the conclusion that I'm opposed to justice; that my tactics must necessarily be opposed to justice; that, therefore he can best serve the ends of justice by blocking me at every turn.

But at least three factors distinguish Mason and his counterparts (prosecutors, police detectives) in this matter.

First, Mason is more keenly aware of the importance of always appreciating the limited scope of the evidence at almost every step in the form of inquiry (up until the final confession). His counterparts often have greater confidence in their certainty about what the evidence (what we have been referring to as posterior evidence) makes probable.

"Doubtless," Mason admitted, "if I knew all the facts, I'd feel differently about it. Doubtless, if Sabin knew all the facts, he'd feel differently about it. You see, he doesn't know all the facts, and there's no likelihood he'll learn them—in time to do the estate any good" (*Perjured Parrot*, p. 123).

Mason's understanding of the shifting nature of evidence in the course of a case prompts him to be more open-minded and questioning than his counterparts.

Second, Mason has an uncanny sense of when persons are being rashly accused of crimes. Here is a dialogue from *The Case of the Perjured Parrot* about Mason's orientation to cases and the accused. The main character in the book whom Mason proves to be innocent is unsure of Mason's methods or interest:

> "What is your interest in me?"
> "You," Mason told her, "are in a spot. My training has been to sympathize with the underdog and fight for him."

### Taking Evidence Personally

"But I'm not an underdog."
"You will be by the time that family gets done with you," said Mason grimly.

Mason's concern for the "underdog" perhaps stems from his sense that the police effort to solve cases as quickly as possible generate a certain likelihood that the evidence will be read by them as convicting someone who turns out to be innocent.

Third, Mason's method in the final stages of an investigation are almost always dialogical—his method culminates in a dialogue in which the guilt and innocence emerges. His counterparts seem bent on their conviction in the absence of confession. Mason is committed to creating a situation in which all of us, using Bayes's theorem, may be enabled to see the probable innocence of his client and the almost certain guilt (in the end) of someone else. As Mason observes: "if you followed my cases, you'll note that most of them have been cleared up in the courtroom. I can suspect the guilty, but about the only way I can really prove my point is by cross-examining witnesses" (pp. 63–64).

Before we hear the words "Objection!" we freely confess that Perry Mason's taking evidence personally is not always successful. Depending on your genre (television, books, movies) his clients are not always innocent, for example. In closing, we only hope that if any readers of this chapter are lawyers who will defend us in court in the future, that you might spend some time with us and conclude that because we are (in your view) persons who are incapable of committing the crimes as charged, there must be some discrepancy between the evidence and the conclusion that we are guilty.

# III

# *Who Is Perry Mason?*

# 9
# Perry Mason, Courtroom Messiah

CHRISTOPHER KETCHAM

There he goes again. A beautiful woman (Sally Fenner) is drowning. And Paul Drake and Perry Mason just happen to be on a fishing trip right where she is and speed their boat to rescue her. Coincidentally she's fleeing from the scene of a murder which she is unaware has been committed ("The Case of the Negligent Nymph," first shown on TV: 12/07/57).

Well, of course the plot is significantly more fluid than that, because she's just stolen a note (out of a message in a bottle prop) from the office of her former boss (George Adler) that incriminates the deceased (George Adler) of murdering his aunt (Agatha Adler). Sally flees with the note after knocking over a lamp but doesn't see George dead on the floor.

In addition to sorting out messages in bottles, rescuing drowning victims, and prying details from an alcoholic widow, Perry Mason must tease out the confession from the actual murderer of the Adlers. Of course, a considerable estate is involved. Chalk up another win for Perry Mason as the widow confesses but needs another drink . . . Hmmm.

Nor is this the only episode where Perry Mason happens to be in the right place at the right time. In "The Case of the Impetuous Imp," Perry again just happens to be on his boat, this time alone, in time to rescue another damsel in distress who also, coincidentally, has a message in a bottle.

And here are a few of the other episodes from the original TV series where Perry just happens to be there, at the right place and time, sometimes while on vacation:

"The Case of the Angry Mourner"

"The Case of the Moth-Eaten Mink"

"The Case of the Fan Dancer's Horse"

"The Case of the Terrified Typist"

"The Case of the Bashful Burro"

"The Case of the Borrowed Baby"

"The Case of the Lurid Letter"

"The Case of a Place Called Midnight"

"The Case of the Feather Cloak"

"The Case of the Fugitive Fraülein"

Perry Mason: Antichrist, the devil, or disciple from God? Well, there's nobody that good, you say. Even Spider-Man has his bad days (remember what happened when he tried to rescue his girlfriend Gwen Stacy and her neck snapped . . . oops); nothing like this could happen to attorney Mason. He's a one-man forensics investigator and infallible defense attorney at the same moment: a Sherlock Holmes and Clarence Darrow all rolled up into one. His questioning of witnesses would make Socrates envious, because, as did the great philosopher, Perry Mason *always* knows the answer . . . but that's what any attorney worth his salt knows, right? Of course, but Perry Mason's record of accomplishment borders on the divine. Well, if you discount his rare losses like "The Case of the Deadly Verdict" but that is only the beginning of the story. Perry doesn't stop there! Or in "The Case of the Dead Ringer" Perry loses a patent case but, of course, the story doesn't conclude with the verdict because there also happens to be a murder.

## The Perry Mason Code

Code junkies, we have cracked the Perry Mason Code. It has taken years of analysis of eighty-odd Perry Mason novels, the TV series, and the movies. From text and anecdotal evidence, we have pieced together the Perry Mason codex which we now present to the world. Scoff not at this work because it is based in fact, not fiction. And fear not—this codex will not be the subject of some alien investigation, or unexplained sightings of Bigfoot . . . for a future History Channel documentary. No, this is being published in the prestigious *Perry Mason Journal of Legal Philosophy* for all the world to profit.

First, let's put to rest that Mason is another Nostradamus. It isn't from the code that we can read the future, but decode the past. Certainly Dan Brown's famous *Da Vinci Code* purports to reveal Mary Magdalene as the Holy Grail, the blood vessel of, chalice for, the receptacle that bears the child of Jesus. Poppycock. Time and disastrous restoration have so marred Leonardo DaVinci's *Last Supper* painting, it's difficult to discern what he actually painted. And we all know that DaVinci experimented with different techniques, sadly with mixed results, including many where he simply walked away, abandoning the work even if it meant the loss of a commission or worse: the wrath of a powerful patron.

Perry Mason would not walk away. Nor, my dear readers, would he ever use an experimental technique that he did not otherwise know would work. Prescient? Many have speculated thus. But like Sherlock Holmes, he's eerily observant and it's, of course, important that he takes cases where he has arrived at just the right time.

## Divine Evidence

We'll not make the case that Perry Mason is the son of God. He has no great sermon to teach us other than justice . . . We may certainly suggest that both biblical love and Perry Mason justice are aspirational. Rather he is God's envoy, the vessel, the chalice, the Holy Grail of justice that scales of evidence weigh out in good and truthful measure.

You see, by the time of Jesus, God had tired of burning bushes and sculpting great stone tablets, sending floods, plagues and other direct interventions. It simply wasn't working. Humans were too headstrong and defiant for these cheap carnival tricks to work anymore. So he sent Jesus down and people began to take a shine to him and his teaching. For those who don't believe that Jesus could be the messiah, take no offense, we're not going there. We'll just be considering Jesus's betrayal and death at the hands of his disciple Judas. And folks, don't rage against this just yet, we're not saying that Judas plunged an actual knife into Jesus or some other such revisionary story about the death of Jesus. No, Judas was a conspiratorial murderer. He turned in the prophet to the authorities for thirty pieces of silver.

Now hold on, you say. What does Perry Mason have to do with all of this—DaVinci, the last supper, Jesus, Judas? Why, he was there, of course. How else do you think that justice was served against the betrayer of Jesus to the executioners of Pontius Pilate? God couldn't go after the Romans. They were heathens, remember. They had a god for every peccadillo, every nuance, and every bit of nastiness. Rather than mess with that manifold dissonance of spiritual meddling, God decided to punish the believer-betrayer Judas in order to send a message to the faithful that God was still around even though God had abandoned (only temporarily as we will see) the rather unproductive plagues and other disasters as the medium of the message.

Perry Mason became the progenitor of justice for the victims of those who defy the commandment, "Thou shalt not kill." As the envoy, the herald from God, Perry Mason shored up belief in the system that produced justice for the victims and families of violent murder whether caused by direct action or conspiracy as was the case for Jesus. And remember, these heathen Romans became faithful followers of Jesus . . . until other bands of heathens came out of the north to plunge Europe into a dark age. More about that in a moment. First, we need to know more about the kind of envoy Perry Mason is.

## What Kind of Envoy Is He?

The hapless prosecutor of the Perry Mason sagas, Hamilton Burger, might have a thing or two to say about his adversary that wouldn't be too charitable, even to call him demon or fallen angel, but that's just plain bitterness showing through. We have done considerable research into the question of what kind of envoy from God Perry Mason is. As he is justice, we first eliminated all of the minions of Satan (a fallen angel in his own right) as bearers of false or tainted information. In turning to the other side, we considered a number of different angelic forms. As a go-between, Perry Mason is an angel. But what kind? Let's review how we deduced that answer.

First, since Perry Mason was around at the time of Christ, the logical order of angels would have been from the Old Testament (the New Testament wasn't written yet, folks). He couldn't have been a Hayyoth, the highest level of angels who hold up the throne of God (this according to the great Jewish scholar Moses Maimonides' (1136–1204) in his *Mishneh Torah*.) Holding up the throne would have kept Perry Mason too busy. Besides, why give Perry Mason that much power? The next level down, the Ophanim are the wheels on Ezekiel's Chariot (Ezekiel: 1). Well, the whole flaming chariot thing with four faced beasts for wheels is a bit bizarre so we don't want to go there to find Perry Mason. So, down to the third level (of ten) we go and we are at Erelim or the courageous ones. Certainly, Perry Mason is courageous in a sense, but he's far craftier than he is a hero. I'm not sure we want to see Perry Mason in tights hefting a broad sword any time soon even in the name of justice.

Next on the list, the Hashmallim are described in terms of lightning . . . nah, not a good fit. Now the Seraphim (Isaiah 6:1–8) are seen flying around the throne of God calling to each other, "Holy, holy, holy." Can't you just see Perry Mason repeating, "Objection, your honor" three times? Besides he doesn't worship the judge, he respects the court. Still not there. But here, one level below the Seraphim are the Malakim, the messengers who visited the patriarchs of the Bible (the really old dudes in the first bible books) as well as many others. Certainly, Perry Mason is more of a messenger, the embodiment of justice, whispering in the ear of the guilty to confess their sins and let the innocent go free. Ah, what a satisfactory feeling it is once we unlock what was thought to have been impenetrable code. Now that's solved, we follow Perry Mason and his contributions to justice across the centuries.

No, wait a minute you say. An angel? Aren't angels, like, part of God. Nope. We will put that right to rest. Our old sage Maimonides was right on that in his *Letter on the Resurrection* where he said that angels were intelligences. They could think on their own. Like junior attorneys, they get their direction from the Managing Partner, but they conduct their own cross-examinations when the great prosecution, the Inquisition, hold forth in Europe between the invasions of Goths, Visigoths, Ostrogoths, and Vandals, and the later enlightening Renaissance.

These inquisitors perverted justice and the whole process of knowing the answer in advance. For example, a favorite torture for women thought to be witches was to dunk (on a ducking stool) them in and out of a pond until they confessed. If the women confessed they were guilty of witchcraft and were then burned at the stake. And if the women drowned in the process they were, quite innocent, praise be to God. In either event, death was preordained. God didn't appreciate this form of justice, as we will see.

It's very disconcerting that God didn't dispatch Perry Mason from wherever he was meting out God's brand of justice to return him to set right the perversion of the infamous inquisition. Instead, God went back to the old ways and set upon the world the plague of the Black Death, spreading it not like the sudden flood of Noah, but let it migrate through the population at its own pace. But, like the flood of Noah or the plagues of Egypt, the result was the same and the population of Europe was so significantly reduced that people began to see that both oppressive churches and repressive nobles simply were not the form of justice they were seeking. Be gone, inquisition!

Please accept our apologies for King and Queen Ferdinand and Isabela of Spain who not only dispatched Christopher Columbus to the new world in 1492, but also expelled Jews and Muslims who would not renounce their religions to become Christian. Sadly, there could be only one Perry Mason who was stretched a bit thin as the population of Europe began to expand its colonial reach around the world. The code hints that at this time of great apostasy he was in Florence, in a dialog with Niccolò Machiavelli (1469–1527) concerning the progress of Machiavelli's work, *The Prince*, to help him understand the need for even-handed justice even in the world of an absolute monarch.

And please also forgive the whole slavery thing in the Americas that got going soon after Columbus arrived. The breaker of slavery, Abraham Lincoln, was not Perry Mason.

Certainly, Lincoln had been a successful attorney, but the war was going rather badly for him and the Union in 1862. What we have discovered in the code is that Perry Mason visited the White House to convince Lincoln of the need to deliver the Emancipation Proclamation. And like he did in all of his courtroom appearances, Perry Mason persuaded Lincoln that he needed to time his proclamation when it would do the most good. In 1862 people were tired of the carnage.

The strong federal government versus states' rights dispute for engaging in war was losing its effectiveness as an argument for continuing the fighting. Perry Mason persuaded Lincoln to engage his cabinet in discussion about justice, the idea of freeing the slaves in both the North and South and declare its so through executive fiat: the Emancipation Proclamation... which Lincoln did, effective January 1st, 1863. Like Perry Mason, Abraham Lincoln changed the argument, changed the focus of the war from an unpopular and obscure concept of governmental power to that of emancipation which reinvigorated the burgeoning abolitionists of the north.

Hey—wait, this wasn't a murder trial, so how does Perry Mason figure into this? Simply, Perry Mason felt a bit sorry for Lincoln. He hated to see a fellow counsel, a brother of the Bar lose so ingloriously. As God's messenger of justice, he used his own powers of persuasion to influence fellow counsel Lincoln to engage the jury of popular opinion at just the right time so that the case for justice could be reinvigorated and the unjustly accused, the slave, would be returned to his rightful place as the innocent victim not the perpetrator of the calamitous and most murderous war.

## This Is So Much Crap and You Know It!

Will you agree with me that a court transcript and resulting written and published decision is probably fairly accurate? And that accuracy improves the more decisions we have? All right then, I will attempt to prove to you that the Perry Mason Code isn't so much crap as you think. Journey with me into the bowels of American jurisprudence for Perry Mason is as visible in the courts as he is (as we have discovered) in his service to God as messenger of justice.

Having perused hundreds of dusty case law digests in the bowels of the local university law library we can say without any reservation that Perry Mason's brand of justice has been distributed throughout American legal jurisprudence. We provide but a few of the hundred or so cases that mention Perry Mason tactics or the great jurist himself. But because the real Perry Mason is not handling the case, a few bumbling imitators get it all wrong to the deprecation of themselves and their hapless clients or prosecutorial targets.

In a question of whether the defendant was properly advised of the consequences and rights of his guilty plea, the court said, "That a defendant may have been tried by a jury in another case or learned of his rights in an earlier plea-taking proceeding would no more negate his right to be informed of the right to and incidents of a trial at the time a plea of guilty is offered than would proof that he had seen Perry Mason on television or read Erle Stanley Gardner." (*Guilty Plea Cases, No. Docket No. 57025, (Calendar No. 2–25.), 235 132* (Mich: Supreme Court 1975).

And in this next case the judge noted in his opinion that loquacious taking of Perry Mason's name in vain tripped up the attorney during Voir Dire, or jury selection questioning, "Mr. Walsh: now, on Perry Mason either the person confessed or someone is going to stand up in the back of the room in two or three days, and say, I did it."

Then the judge noted that the prosecutor said "Okay, now obviously most cases aren't like that. And there is not a confession in this case. Would anyone believe that this individual could not have committed the crime, simply because he did not confess to that crime?" (*Jackson v. State, No. No. 82–1843, 453 456* (Fla: Dist. Court of Appeals, 4th Dist. 1984)). Then the judge noted that the bumbling boob of a prosecutor tried the same tactic when questioning the same witness. On appeal the defendant was given a new trial. One does not mess with Perry Mason's impeccable track record by poor imitation.

Yet another prosecutor did try to bring in the peerless Perry Mason: "Defendant also alleges that the prosecutor improperly argued in response to a defense counsel statement that she was not Perry Mason, as follows: 'As I recall, all of Perry Mason's clients were not guilty, and you didn't hear her say that Dan didn't do it'." (*State v. Basile, No. No. 77123,*

942 342 (Mo: Supreme Court 1997)). Well, the defense's motion for mistrial failed anyway.

This next prosecutor is simply priceless. The judge notes in his opinion that, "The prosecutor also persistently disparaged the defense case, remarking that the defense was following a 'script' that was 'like right out of Perry Mason'. Continuing with this theme, the prosecutor accused the defense of manufacturing certain evidence, and claimed that the defense witness who confessed to the robbery had 'perjur[ed] himself', and was 'more full of crap than a Christmas turkey'." (*People v. Robinson, 260 AD 2d 508—NY: Appellate Div., 2nd Dept. 1999*).

Turning to defense counsels now, this one tried a Perry Mason tactic but without knowing all the answers, and guess what happened next. The judge recorded that, "In a Perry Mason like manner, defense counsel filed a motion for a new trial upon the grounds of newly-discovered evidence—such evidence being that of a person who was with the assailant, and who allegedly would testify that another person was the assailant. Unfortunately for defense counsel, they have encountered an obstacle which Perry Mason never was forced to overcome. Although the witness talked to defense counsel, he refused to testify before the court, asserting, instead, the privilege against self-incrimination" (*State v. Broady, No. 74AP-149, 41 17* (Ohio: Court of Appeals 1974)).

Here a judge tried to inform the jury about what reasonable doubt is and unfairly disparaged Perry Mason at the same time which is why the case was appealed, "This is not Perry Mason. Perhaps some of you have seen defendants stand right up and say 'I did it', or 'I didn't do it'. Forget about that; that is for entertainment purposes, that doesn't occur. At least from my experiences in the law I have yet to see anyone get up from the back of the Courtroom and say 'I'm guilty and the defendant is not'. Forget that. This is a very very serious crime." (*State v. McKeough, 300 755* (Me: Supreme Judicial Court 1973)).

And sometimes attorneys get slapped even when they say something out of earshot of the jury. Here the judge records that out of earshot of the jury the prosecutor said, "I think the record should reflect that that statement was made in light of a question posed to that same witness immediately prior to it being posed, and that is a statement made by myself that what you see on television isn't exactly the way it occurs, something like that, that this isn't like a Perry Mason television set and I said Mr. Garaas may—I did not say the defendant was not going to jump up. I said someone or anyone or a person, however it was worded, will not get up and say, 'I did it'." (*State v. Skjonsby, No. Cr. No. 749-A, 319 764* (ND: Supreme Court 1982)).

In this next case the defense counsel did one of the celebrated substitution routines made famous in Perry Mason trials, but which went horribly wrong, "In pseudo-Perry Mason style, defense counsel substitutes a look-alike sister for the female co-defendant at the counsel table during the noon recess; the sister puts on the defendant's blazer and the defendant sits in the back of the courtroom. The witness, a police officer who that morning made a critical in-court identification on direct examination, is then led to say on cross-examination that he sees the same people in the courtroom. Asked "Where are they?" the witness replies, "Seated at the [defense] table." (*United States of America, Appellee, v. Elizabeth SABATER, Appellant. No. 1227, Docket 87–1010.* (United States Court of Appeals, Second Circuit)). The appellate court did not find this tactic amusing.

It isn't just the lawyers who see visions of Perry Mason. Here the defendant asked to have the same attorney who represented him at trial to represent him at his sentencing. However the defendant saw in female counsel the likeness of Perry Mason:

> THE COURT: So, you think that she is competent and you should have her represent you?
>
> THE DEFENDANT: There is no question from the start she is competent.
>
> THE COURT: And you have no questions as to her loyalty towards you or her ability to act?
>
> THE DEFENDANT: At this stage, your honor, my memory is exhausted, I think she is Perry Mason now.

The circuit court did reappoint the female attorney who now looked like Perry Mason to the defendant. (*People v. Coleman, 544 NE 2d 330–Ill: Supreme Court 1989*).

And finally, you have to do it right to be a Perry Mason. You just can't wing it and hope to succeed. Here the judge noted that the prosecutor used Perry Mason tactics unwisely. "These tactics were unwise and unnecessary. Although we might expect a character in a Perry Mason melodrama to point to a defendant and brand him a liar, such conduct is inconsistent with the duty of the prosecutor to 'seek justice, not merely to convict" (ABA Code of Professional Responsibility, Final Draft, 1969, Ethical Consideration 7–13, at 79. See H. Drinker, Legal Ethics 148 (1953)." *United States v. White, 486 F. 2d 204—Court of Appeals, 2nd Circuit 1973.*[1]

Yes, to seek justice is what Perry Mason does, not just a finding of not guilty for his client. So, you see, jurists must be careful to avoid trying to imitate the likes of Perry Mason without possessing his considerable investigative and courtroom skills, or take his name in vain (the vengeful messenger from God thing).

## Back at the Last Supper

We're not saying that the murder of Jesus was Perry Mason's first case, but it certainly was very early in his career. That's why it's a bit less documented than his later successes. Perry Mason isn't mentioned by name anywhere in the Bible nor has he any discernable presence, even with x-ray analysis of DaVinci's Last Supper or other paintings or works of the same. But that's the beauty of the code. God knew that nobody at the time of Jesus would believe someone like Perry

---

[1] Other cases where Mason's name is mentioned include: US v. Hinkson, 585 F. 3d 1247—Court of Appeals, 9th Circuit 2009; Williams v. State, 658 P. 2d 499—Okla: Court of Criminal Appeals 1983; State v. Martin, 103 Ohio St. 3d 385—Ohio: Supreme Court 2004; State v. Burgins, 44 Ohio App. 3d 158—Ohio: Court of Appeals 1988; State v. Roth, 549 SW 2d 652—Mo: Court of Appeals 1977; People v. Crawford, 253 Cal. App. 2d 524—Cal: Court of Appeal, 5th Appellate Dist. 1967; Freeman v. Leapley, 519 NW 2d 615—SD: Supreme Court 1994; State v. Reado, 472 So. 2d 271—La: Court of Appeals, 1st Circuit 1985; Kincek v. Hall, 175 P. 3d 496—Or. Court of Appeals 2007; State v. Schaffer, 454 SW 2d 60—Mo: Supreme Court, 2nd Div. 1970; United States v. Bostic, 360 F. Supp. 1305—Dist. Court, ED Pennsylvania 1973; People v. Castillo, Cal: Court of Appeal, 4th Appellate Dist., 2nd Div. 2007; State v. Moten, Tenn: Court of Criminal Appeals 2006; Pannell v. State, 455 So. 2d 785—Miss: Supreme Court 1984; Starkey v. State, 704 SW 2d 805—Tex: Court of Appeals, 5th Dist. 1985.

Mason could exist and God really didn't want someone else that powerful ideologically to compete with Jesus. Such a contest would have proved ultimately disastrous, possibly even splitting the faithful into even more splinter groups than Jews, Christians, and the later Muslims and all their myriad of sects. And, of course, we must also remember that at the time of Jesus the dominant form of justice was Roman and it was brutal, unyielding, and subject to considerable oppressive force. For God, one martyr was enough. And God could see uses for someone who works behind the scenes in the courtroom rather than in the limelight of politics or theology. By preventing injustice, justice would be served.

This idea isn't something radical or new as were the gospels from the prophets Abraham, Moses, Jesus, and Mohammed. It was more subtle and messed less with the prevailing ideologies of the time, but it was always couched in justice.

While we don't believe that God plants the idea that Perry Mason needs to be at such and such a place at such and such a time (remember Maimonides), God did give him the ability for uncanny timing (which is self-evident in his twentieth and twenty-first century courtroom activities). We still don't know for certain how Perry Mason came to arrive at (more like near) the last supper. However, we have some still fuzzy logic indices and tentative algorithms that lean towards the idea that he was lodging nearby and he overheard Jesus explain to his disciples that someone would deny him three times and someone would betray him. So, as we see it, Perry Mason hung around the back alley to better observe the proceedings, perhaps through an open door or window (the stench must have been horrific in the sewer that was the back alley). The whole body and blood thing likely would have been disconcerting to Perry Mason but he would have at least understood these notions metaphorically, even though he would later realize how predictive this was of Jesus's eventual death.

Certainly we all know the story that Jesus knew that Judas would betray him to the authorities with a kiss (Matthew 26:47). And once the kiss was offered, the authorities trundled Jesus away. But we also know that Judas had second thoughts and tried to return to the priests and elders the thirty pieces of silver he had received for his treason (Matthew 27:3). In the Gospel of Matthew, Judas throws the pieces of silver into the temple and goes off to commit suicide.

What the Bible doesn't tell us is how Judas came to have these second thoughts (nope, not in Matthew, nor Mark, nor Luke). You are correct if you guess that Perry Mason was at the ready, before the court of justice where he had cornered Judas in a lonesome docket, questioning him mercilessly in his own inimitable way until Judas recanted his innocence and admitted his guilt. But since the only 'official' court in Jerusalem at the time was Roman and they were delighted with Judas for having delivered Jesus unto them, Perry Mason knew that not only would he have to get Judas to admit guilt, which is his normal modus operandi, but also, in order to avenge Jesus's death, he would have to convince Judas to accept his penance for murder: first by return all the blood money, and; second, (the more difficult)convincing him to administer his own capital punishment. Justice was done. Some say this was Perry Mason's finest hour.

# 10
# Trust and Temptation at the Office

ALEXANDER E. HOOKE

> Perry, you're a cross between a boy and a philosopher, an impractical, hard-hitting visionary, a damned altruistic cynic, a credulous skeptic . . . and dammit, how I envy you your outlook on life!
>
> —PAUL DRAKE, *The Case of the Caretaker's Cat*, p. 143

> No, Della . . . A lawyer isn't like a shopkeeper who can sell his wares or not as he chooses. He holds his talents in trust for the unfortunate.
>
> —PERRY MASON, *The Case of the Caretaker's Cat*, p. 4

> "That's not an orthodox way of practicing law," Della Street pointed out. "Who the hell wants to be orthodox?" Mason grinned.
>
> —*The Case of the Caretaker's Cat*, p. 110

There actually was a moment when Perry Mason proposed marriage to Della Street. For the millions of fans of the books or televisions shows, this could have sparked a moment for celebration and curiosity. So many of them have been speculating or anticipating a steamy romance or eventual matrimony for the renowned lawyer and his faithful secretary.

Alas, the proposal was a ruse. Perry needs Della to go on a mock honeymoon so the lawyer can conduct his own investigation. Della plays along, with bemusement and wonder. She teases Perry over how much she should pretend they are newly-weds. Imagine the scene. A handsome and successful lawyer sharing quarters at an exclusive mountain hotel with a beautiful and sharp assistant. No one notices them registering as Mr. and Mrs. Watson Clammert. The temptation for a liaison, in the eyes of a Perry Mason fan, was overwhelming.

Temptation is an enduring feature in detective and criminal stories. Indeed, without humans being driven by such appetites as an endless taste for easy money, wounded pride, lingering vengeance, relentless lust, among so many other vices that underscore human behavior, this genre of writing and film-making have left no mark on popular culture. Most of the cases Perry Mason takes on involve individuals who are wealthy—by inheritance, smarts, hard work or good luck. Their crimes that solicit the attention of the best-known lawyer in California have little to do with survival, such as finding a place to sleep or begging for the next meal. They mostly emerge in scenes with mansions, mountain villas, vacation resorts or yachts.

While the vagaries and powers of temptation are central to crime stories, Perry Mason creator Erle Stanley Gardner envisioned a distinct angle. He did this when nearly all of the popular detective and crime stories of the 1930s and 1940s featured the lone wolf. It was one man against a dark and sinister world. Police were corrupt, women were femme fatales, men were scheming Lotharios, tycoons manipulated anyone, and no matter how innocent people seemed it was best to assume they were concealing a sinister plan or malicious desire.

Dashiell Hammett's *The Maltese Falcon* is often credited for setting the standard of crime writing as a potential art form rather than mere pulp fiction. Within ten years of its publication, *The Maltese Falcon* was turned into three different movies, including the classic version starring Humphrey Bogart as detective Sam Spade. While Hollywood censors were able to tone down or eliminate some of the more lascivious moments for viewers, to readers it is quite clear that Spade is not much different from his clients and their antagonists.

Hammett, a private eye turned novelist, shows that Spade has occasional dalliances with his secretary, maintains an on-going affair with his partner's wife, not to mention a quick and intense romance with the ultimate villain of the story—his own client. Can I pay you with my body, she bluntly asks him. Sam Spade is not free of the temptations. He fights with the police, slaps around gunslingers, seduces vulnerable women, and is suspicious of anyone. Sam Spade, like subsequent heroes as dissimilar as Jason Bourne, Spider Man, and Indiana Jones, is the model of the lone wolf. No one can be trusted.

For Erle Stanley Gardner, a lawyer turned novelist, Perry Mason embraces an implicit trust as a potential counter to such a cynical outlook. This trust is found in the collaboration, friendship and professional collegiality of Perry, Della, and Paul Drake, Mason's primary detective. Perry's legal skills and regional fame, Della's resourcefulness and beauty, and Paul's shrewdness and persistence, could easily have been the bases for pursuing personal and selfish gains whenever a case arose, particularly with the numerous hefty fees and bribes offered by miscreant millionaires.

In light of the competitive nature of criminal justice as a kind of game among established adversaries (prosecutors, defense attorneys, police, and judges), there is the temptation to circumvent the law in order to win one's case. Mason admits this often. "Legality be damned" or a similar phrase is uttered when it comes to properly defending his client This attitude often puts Della and Paul in danger. In *The Case of the Silent Partner,* Perry risks Della being arrested as a witness or accomplice to a crime. He frequently requests a furtive task from Paul that could have the Drake Detective Agency lose its license. Throughout there is an implicit trust among the three that gives them the courage to momentarily suspend self-interest and share the battle to win the case.

American philosopher Alphonso Lingis often speaks of the importance of trust and courage when we encounter a stranger. Trust is not based on a deliberative and negotiated signed agreement that outlines each party's duty and possible punishment for violating the contract. It is anchored to something more immediate and implicit. To trust someone without any promise or guarantee, without one's long-term interests calculated, takes an element of nerve or guts. Lingis's observations could easily apply to scenarios when even people with whom we are familiar may be hiding or disguising something. "In trust one adheres to something one sees only partially or unclearly or understands only vaguely or ambiguously. . . . Trust is a break, a cut made in the extending map of certainties and probabilities" (*Trust*, pp. 64–65). Trust enables Perry, Della, and Paul to break from the map of mutual suspicion and selfish calculation so that they can together pursue something more important—justice and their client's best interests.

## The Secretary

> The private constitutes, along with the sacred, that portion of human experience for which secrecy is most indispensible.
>
> —SISSELA BOK, *Secrets*

Businesses and institutions no longer list jobs for 'secretaries'. Now they deploy bureaucratic euphemisms to hire women—administrative assistants, office technicians or special technology aides. This devaluation of the term 'secretary' betrays a lack of respect and understanding of an essential component of a profession.

As its etymology indicates, the secretary is a bearer of secrets. Being *discreet*, *secreting* information, *discerning* the right action or person for the right times all share the roots of secretary. Long before computers and data processors, secretaries have always been the center of information. Gossip, inner workings of the organization, rumors and speculations, questionable decisions and eye-raising hearsay all flow through her desk. She is both a great source of knowledge and also a master of secrecy. While most professionals are paid for their knowledge and the ability to convey or publicize their insights reflecting such knowledge, the secretary finds that the more she knows the more she must conceal. The secretary must function in this paradoxical position, hence the trust placed in her.

Della Street embodies this paradox. In the novels Erle Stanley Gardner frequently lists the cast of characters before the reader starts Chapter 1. Here is a sampling of his introductions to Della: "beautiful and brainy," "Mason's secretary, co-conspirator, and generally a good gal in a pinch," "tried and true, she had her own special niche." Throughout the plots Della is her chief's confidante, acute observer of witnesses or suspects ready to provide insights about their personalities that Perry might have missed, and a sounding board for Perry's schemes and reflections about the nature of law and crime.

In *The Case of the Silent Partner* Perry needs Della to put on a disguise that resembles a potential client, learn to sign her signatures, take her traveler's checks and cash them at different business venues. It clearly seems that Perry is asking Della to commit forgery and fraud, if not hindering a police investigation to a murder. They both know that if the scheme falters, Perry will next meet Della not at the office but in jail for her actions. Knowing they are pushing the boundaries, he apologizes for the danger. "I hate to do this, Della. If there's been anyone else I could trust..."

In *The Case of the Caretaker's Cat,* Perry and Della fake an elopement in order to find details about potential suspects, including their possible motives or alibis. The secretary winds up being her boss's decoy, driver, accomplice, and scout. When the bellhop at the hotel's front desk delivers a surprise message to Mason that he is expected to be in New York during the honeymoon night, Della cuts up an onion so her eyes can start weeping, then stages a mock broken-hearted scene, saying to her "husband," "You d-d-d-don't l-l-love me." Her romantic playfulness confuses Mason as well as the reader, wondering if she is being sincere or testing Mason on how well he enjoys faking the honeymoon.

Gardner himself became annoyed with the constant speculation on a romance or marriage between Perry and Della. He found his fans somewhat fickle on this issue. "Those who want Della to sleep with her boss are the ones who are afraid she isn't, and those who think she shouldn't are the ones who are certain she is." We have emphasized the novels so far, for in the television shows the relationship between the lawyer and his secretary is exemplary but sanitized. As presented by Raymond Burr and Barbara Hale, the suggestive and playful nuances and ambiguities were largely absent on screen. The books show them smoking cigarettes, mildly cursing, Perry calling Della in the middle of the night as if she has no personal life, Paul suggestively teasing over why they just don't get married. When Perry and Della, in *The*

*Alexander E. Hooke*

*Case of the Rolling Bones,* interrupt Paul's sleep twice in one night, Paul blurts, "You again! Why don't you go on and make whoopee? . . . and let working men get a decent night's sleep?" This bantering and friendly joking contribute to rather than distract their shared commitment to Perry's client.

Had Perry and Della become lovers or husband and wife, this would have weakened, in Gardner's view, the lawyer's sex appeal. Such a development would also cloud their discerning abilities when it came to making the smartest decisions about handling a case. Their affection for one another could easily jeopardize their collaborative efforts in pursuing justice. It's no accident that romantic or sexual developments in professional life have endured as moral and institutional controversies.

Gardner is not entirely innocent, though. He did fuel his fans' ongoing speculations. After two non-stop days on a case, there's a scene in *The Case of the Daring Decoy* where Perry insists he follow Della home in his car as he was worried about her driving alone in the late night. As they reach her apartment, Della tells Perry, "Custom decrees that when a man has taken a girl home, he is entitled to a token of thanks." She then plants a full kiss on his lips.

At the end of *The Case of the Half-Awakened Wife,* where a beautiful 400-acre estate isolated in the tranquil woods of California was central to a case, Perry and Della reflect on how their client was found not guilty. Then Perry picks up the newspaper and sees the property is for sale. He looks to Della and suggests they buy the land in her name. He then adds, "We could have it for a little hideaway. I could put up a bungalow out under those trees back from the lake. Perhaps someday . . ." Perry adds without finishing the sentence. He looks out the window with dreamy eyes while Della closes the novel smiling, "Go ahead chief. Even if you are just day dreaming. It's a swell idea."

## The Private Eye

The eye, be it strange, vague, or simply beautiful, has always been, and still is, among the civilized as among the primitives, the doorway for evil influences.

GEORGES BATAILLE, *Critical Dictionary*

## Trust and Temptation at the Office

The private eye, someone who investigates people's personal lives outside the authority of the police or state, has an uneven history. It began as an effort by people hiring talented detectives to find information about counterfeiters, frauds, blackmailers, among other nefarious types adroit in cheating and scamming while eluding the tentacles of the law.

The Pinkerton Agency of the late nineteenth century was probably the first formal and profitable group to offer detective services on a systematic and reliable scale. Sometimes the agents turned into insular groups who sold their skills and services as hired hands. They would be employed by corporations and businesses to disrupt efforts at unionizing workers or spark riots and violence should peaceful protests arise. In any event, the symbol of the Pinkertons was an eyeball cast in a furtive glance. It meant that those who engage a Pinkerton are having someone do their looking any time of day or night, or, in today's parlance, 24/7.

Paul Drake, head of the Drake Detective Agency, could easily have this symbol above his office's entrance. He generally keeps regular hours, though there is no hour of the day or night when he is unavailable to Perry Mason. If by chance Paul is occupied for the moment—he is known to be a ladies' man, but few specifics are provided—he will immediately contact one or two of his operatives who are on call. In his apartment Perry Mason has a private phone with an unlisted number. Only two people on the planet know this number—Della Street and Paul Drake.

Unlike the relationship between Perry and Della—where the novels are much more subtle—the one between Perry and Paul is captured fairly well in both literary and screen venues. Paul is tall, handsome, can easily handle himself if anyone tries to get rough with him. He avoids physical confrontations since his main task is to provide Perry some important information as quickly as possible, particularly if this information is still unknown to police and prosecutors.

A scene in *The Case of the Angry Mourner* is fairly typical. Perry departs for a weekend retreat at a cabin resort. Someone at the resort is found murdered. Perry suddenly becomes involved, phones Paul Drake in the middle of the night and asks him to take a private plane immediately to the resort. Without shaving or eating, Paul arrives before dawn to start the case, hours before anyone else begins investigating the crime.

As with Della, Paul can be a sounding board for Perry. In *The Case of the Sulky Girl,* the second Perry Mason novel, Paul already pushes Perry to review his options of pursuing a case and offers possible obstacles. Perry needs to tail a possible suspect or witness, but one who is somewhat clever and resourceful. Paul introduces the rough shadow scheme. Perry has heard of this but unsure of its exact nature. It's a detective trick where the target is followed by two private eyes, he knows it, and winds up confiding to the first detective out of greater fear of the second. "We don't ordinarily talk about it—not to outsiders, anyway," Paul tells Perry. Then he trusts Perry as an insider and details the psychological mechanics that often make rough shadow scheme succeed.

A good detective lives an unusual paradox. Whereas the good secretary has to conceal all she knows except to her boss, a reliable detective has to conceal himself. As Gardner introduces him, Paul Drake is a "detective who tried not to look like one," or "he always looked disinterested and so succeeded in fooling the public." The reader learns that Paul has three phones in his bedroom (in a time of only landline phones with no caller ID), so he can receive instructions from Perry and reach his operatives at the same time. Oddly, while good detectives try to look like a typical person, their eating and sleeping routines are quite atypical. As Drake jests about the private eye, "If he has brains, it helps. But they're not *really* necessary."

The audience's understandable rejoinder: Then what does a detective look like? Think of your favorite detectives and none of them looks like a detective. But Gardner's quip plays on the mind of the viewer in terms of what he or she expected in trying to spot a detective. The eye of the Perry Mason fan is no match for the observant powers of Paul Drake. Hence, the better the detective, the less we can detect him. For this reason Paul Drake, partly unseen, is central to the work of Perry Mason.

## The Defense Attorney

Lawyer. n. One skilled in circumvention of the law.

—AMBROSE BIERCE, *The Devil's Dictionary*

## Trust and Temptation at the Office

The legal profession functions with an ambivalent perspective on laws. First, laws provide the framework for living in a democracy and respecting the rights and freedoms of one another. Second, they can be construed as rules that are vague, loosely or inconsistently enforced, subject to change or contrasting interpretations by legislators, politicians, wordsmiths, and everyday citizens.

Third, laws provide the basic dictates in the game of crime, much like rules of an election or sporting contest. In an adversarial climate, epitomized in the bedrock axiom "everyone is innocent until proven guilty," the most accomplished figures in our system of justice are competitors. Just as notable athletes like Babe Ruth, Muhammad Ali, Tom Brady, or Earl Monroe compete at a level where they play by the rules while testing their limits in order to win the game, talented lawyers abide by the laws while always prepared to challenge their limits in order to win the case.

Perry Mason works at that level. His combativeness is clearly evident in both literary and visual venues. His battles with prosecutors, the police, witnesses, news reporters (in the novels the daily newspapers were often interviewing Mason) are legendary. The television series features numerous battles with Lieutenant Tragg, chief police investigator, and Hamilton Burger, district attorney and prosecutor. While Perry Mason television fans insist he never lost a case (one possible defeat is discounted as Raymond Burr did not appear in the show), in the novels he is somewhat more contrite. Ruminating with Della about which client to take in *The Case of the Silent Partner,* Perry humbly admits to his confidante. "I'm not infallible. My percentage should run about fifty-fifty. So far I've always been on the black side of the ledger. That's luck."

Mason also has a soft spot for the underdog. *The Case of the Rolling Bones* begins with Mason ruminating with Della on the difference between his wealthy and poor clients. "Rich people worry too much ... They stew up a high blood pressure over a one-point drop in the interest rate. Poor people get right down to brass tacks: love, hunger, murder. . . ." While his wealthier clients provide a substantial living for Mason and those who work with him, readers and viewers will also find him charging a token one-dollar fee to an elderly client with little money, defending an old friend who can't afford an attorney, giving Della a $20,000 check for one of her close friends who is in serious trouble and no questions asked.

The notion that the hero must always win and never fail is part of folklore and fiction. In real life, if someone always wins then either the contest is rigged, as with casino gambling, or it's an inherently uneven playing field in which one contestant is forbidden to win. Still, from Sam Spade to Columbo and Bones, victory inevitably appears at the end. That feature is for devoted fans. Parenthetically, Mason and Burger, as we often find with exceptional athletes, were actually respectful of one another. Mason read one of Burger's scholarly publications to prepare his defense. After Mason's victory, Burger asks Mason about his key tactic on a subtle point in law. Mason then recites a short passage from Burger's own writing.

Mason maintains a tacit hierarchy of obligations. First is the duty to share the truth with witnesses and reporters. Then he is expected to co-operate with police, investigators, and those he suspects having the real motive and opportunity to commit the murder. Next is respecting law and the legal profession. Mason is somewhat famous. When he travels people recognize his name. Bellhops and waitresses occasionally ask for his autograph; at a restaurant or night club patrons might interrupt him with a question or compliment. He is careful not to let this public stature detract from properly representing the profession.

It is tempting to state the obvious by claiming Mason's client lies at the top of this hierarchy of obligations. Doesn't every professional say this? The doctor claims to focus on everything that helps a patient; for the teacher only the student matters; the priest is devoted to each parishioner. Yet such lofty ideals are easily corrupted by temptations that appeal to professionals working in isolation or self-serving circumstances. They reflect the human beings they serve. At the same time the professional, in this case the lawyer, secretary and detective, must suspend these temptations for the good of the cause.

## Collaborations and Friendships

Before the powers of temptation, few are strong enough to go it alone. Most of us could use the insights of another to air out our shortcomings and weaknesses. More importantly, most of us need to trust others to accomplish worthy projects and endeavors that could be endangered by our vices.

Even the most devoted fan can see that for Perry Mason, whose wealth and public reputation could incite the most devilish temptations for many, the lone wolf is an exaggerated myth. As the introductory epigraphs from *The Case of the Caretaker's Cat* indicate, it is clear that Perry Mason embraces contradictions within his own life, he eschews the orthodox, and wants to help those unfortunates accused of a crime he believes they did not commit. No doubt he likes the hefty fee from a wealthy client.

Yet his fundamental imperative is to ensure that justice has been done, primarily for his client. To abide by this imperative, Perry Mason has two other individuals at the top of his hierarchy. They are collaborators and friends. Two he can trust without qualification—Della Street and Paul Drake.

# 11
# When Is a Lawyer Not a Lawyer?

JOHN V. KARAVITIS

Perry Mason is a fictional defense attorney whose name is synonymous with brilliant legal defense, due process of law, and the inevitable discovery of the true identity of the murderer. Created by Erle Stanley Gardner, a real-life attorney with two decades of experience practicing law in the state of California, Perry Mason has appeared in every conceivable medium: radio, television, movies, and even comic books. But the character is best known from the 271-episode CBS television series which lasted from 1957 to 1966, with Raymond Burr starring as the indefatigable legal knight in shining armor.

The plot nearly always follows a predictable formula, in two parts. In the first part, a stressful situation results in a murder; and the police arrest the prime suspect, who invariably becomes Perry Mason's client. In the second part, typically at a preliminary hearing, Perry Mason's diligent and relentless pursuit of the truth results in the discovery of the true murderer, and the exoneration and release of his client.

For those of you who remember this television series, you might be wondering by now where this chapter could be headed. Perry Mason is just a lawyer, isn't he? And the plot formula rarely deviates from its established two-part pattern. What philosophy could there be in *Perry Mason*? To get an answer, I decided to do what Perry Mason himself would have done. I let the facts speak for themselves.

John V. Karavitis

## Let's Start with the Facts

In every episode, Perry Mason finds himself defending a client who has been accused of murder. One of the important activities that occurs even before his client's arrest is the search for information. This search for information is motivated by the client's immediate situation, and by the desire to get to the truth. Who really committed the murder, and why?

A defense lawyer like Perry Mason is involved in the search for truth. He's trying to understand what really happened, and he has to cover a lot of ground in order to get to it. He finds himself with a constellation of facts which either initially contradict each other, or worse, do not seem to be connected at all. He has to deal with clients and witnesses who may, for various reasons, be unwilling to reveal what they know. And he also has to deal with the police and the district attorney, who may independently discover facts which lead them to believe that Perry Mason's client is guilty. Helping him in his search for the truth is private detective Paul Drake. Mason's confidential secretary, Della Street, also does her part in his search for the truth, especially when she accompanies Perry Mason out in the field on his own investigative efforts.

So Perry Mason is on a search for the truth. But to get to the truth, he has to obtain knowledge of the events that led to the murder. Epistemology is the branch of philosophy that deals with knowledge, and when a statement about the world can be considered to be true. The definition we have of what can be considered to be knowledge comes from *Theaetetus*, one of the works of Plato (429–347 B.C.E.). In this dialog, we have Socrates and Theaetetus discussing the nature of knowledge. At the end, we're left with the definition of knowledge as *justified true belief*. A statement about the world can be considered knowledge if 1. the statement is true, 2. we believe it to be true, and 3. we're justified in our belief in it. And we can consider ourselves to be justified about a belief if we have evidence for it.

Philosophers have two ways of thinking about the truth. The first is the correspondence theory of truth. This theory says that a claim about the world is true if it accurately describes the world. The second is the coherence theory of truth. This theory says that a claim about the world is true if it makes sense with respect to other statements about the world. When Perry Mason is investigating the circumstances of a murder, he finds himself following both theories of the truth. He wants facts that accurately describe the events leading up to the murder. But he also wants facts that make coherent sense with each other.

If a newly discovered "fact" doesn't agree with everything else that has been considered to be the truth up to this point, then one of two situations must exist. Either this new fact is not really a fact or the story told to date by all of the previously ascertained facts is not the one that correctly explains the murder. Either way, something has to give. Throughout each episode, we see Perry Mason go through this iterative process: from facts to theory, to new facts, to revised and updated theory, right up until the very end. Perry Mason, in his search for the truth, relies on both the correspondence theory of truth and the coherence theory of truth.

When we see Perry Mason work toward discovering the truth, we superficially see a lawyer doing what has to be done to prove the innocence of his client. But on a deeper level, what Perry Mason is doing is recreating the recent past. So, Perry Mason isn't just a trial lawyer. Perry Mason is also a *historian*.

## From Historical Evidence to the Truth

At this point, you may be rolling your eyes. You may think, in the words of Hamilton Burger, that I'm engaging in a "wild-eyed, dramatic grandstand play" ("The Case of the Terrified Typist"). Or I've tricked you by crafting a chapter "which is pure poppycock! Absolute and complete nonsense" ("The Case of the Shapely Shadow"). But what Perry Mason is doing is in fact what historians do.

History is the narrative that tells us what happened in the past, and why. And historians have to deal with the same obstacles that defense attorneys face. Just as Perry Mason goes up against the explanation of events that the police have crafted which results in the presumed guilt and arrest of his client, historians frequently have to deal with an established and well-accepted story about the past.

District Attorney Hamilton Burger eloquently and succinctly states the purpose of his office. "Your Honor, the District Attorney's office functions to determine the truth, and to prosecute the guilty" ("The Case of the Prodigal Parent"). But curiously, the prosecution always seems to arrive at a determination of guilt almost immediately, and stops at the obvious. Once the prosecution decides that the prime suspect is guilty of murder, all subsequent efforts, if any, are biased by this presumption. Lieutenant Arthur Tragg explains to Perry Mason why they believe his client is guilty. "Well, he's got the kind of story we're looking for" ("The Case of the Vagabond Vixen"). Hamilton Burger invariably asserts his belief in the strength of the evidence that makes up his case. "It will do—nicely," he informs Perry Mason. ("The Case of the Crimson Kiss"). When confronted by a change in a witness's belief as to who killed her husband, the district attorney stands his ground. "Well, even so . . . On the basis of our evidence there's almost no doubt that . . ." ("The Case of the Lonely Heiress").

But perhaps the most direct explanation for the speed and certainty with which the prosecution concludes who the guilty party is relies on the issue of circumstantial evidence. District Attorney Burger explains his position to a person of interest who claims to have evidence in a murder case. "We're preparing to take our case into court. It's a circumstantial case, but we've found that circumstances are frequently more reliable and less controversial than witnesses" ("The Case of the Golden Fraud"). In another episode, Sheriff Gene Norris, an old friend of Perry Mason's, expresses the same faith in circumstantial evidence after the murder of his daughter. Perry Mason asks his friend, "You're not letting circumstances build up something in your mind, are you, Gene?" Sheriff Norris replies angrily. "Sure, circumstances that make up evidence! Facts that add in!" ("The Case of the Violent Village").

But Perry Mason refuses to accept their version of the truth, and he relentlessly pursues every possible lead. "I always believe my client," he tells Lieutenant Tragg ("The Case of the Restless Redhead"). Perry Mason gathers evidence from many different sources: documentation; physical evidence (bullets, fingerprints, blood spatters); eyewitness

## When Is a Lawyer Not a Lawyer?

testimony from individuals hostile to his client, and sometimes from clients themselves who are holding back crucial facts. "What else haven't you told me?" is a typical Mason question to a client ("The Case of the Nimble Nephew"). He then crafts a narrative which takes all of the evidence that has been discovered to date and presents what he believes to be the truth. This narrative has to be strong enough to overturn the story that the District Attorney is relying upon.

And Mason doesn't arrive at the truth on his first attempt. He arrives at the truth in an iterative fashion: from facts to theory, to new facts, and then to a revised and updated theory. Perry Mason is willing to change his view of reality as the facts dictate. "There's a law of logic that says, 'If you're searching for the truth, you sometimes have to look for the illogical'." ("The Case of the Nimble Nephew"). Each revised theory is a new perspective of recent history which brings Perry Mason closer to what really happened, and why. This is exactly what historians do.

The more astute reader of this chapter may now be eagerly thinking that he can quickly refute my claim. He would no doubt point out that Perry Mason, on numerous occasions, has clearly interfered with what I would call the history of the case. Perry Mason appears to be doing so when he instructs his client to do something after the murder has occurred, or when he himself gets personally involved, seemingly to tamper with evidence. For example, when he makes a notch in the barrel of a .38 Colt snub-nosed revolver that his client found in her apartment ("The Case of the Restless Redhead"); or when he tears up a taxicab receipt and instructs his client to use subterfuge to obtain a second taxicab fare receipt in the same amount ("The Case of the Nervous Accomplice"). But as these events occur after the murder, they only appear to be a case of interfering with the history of the case. Rather, these are methods that Perry Mason uses to assertively cast doubt on the presumptive claims of the prosecution, or on the reliability of witnesses.

So, although the prosecution and Perry Mason both act as historians of the recent past, they each have different perspectives on reality. Their perspectives color their efforts in the search for the truth. The district attorney stops searching for the truth the first moment that the facts paint Perry

Mason's client as the murderer. It is a view of reality that takes the facts to date—the circumstances—at face value. Perry Mason, on the other hand, never accepts anything at face value. On the one hand, he does not need to. He is certain that his efforts will inevitably bring out the truth. On the other hand, he cannot. He has to defend his client to the best of his ability.

## Motive! Motive! Motive!

Still not convinced? There's one final piece to my argument that I think will make things crystal clear. Defense lawyers have to convince the court, and the jury if need be, that not only does the physical evidence fail to prove that their client is guilty, but also that their client had no motive to commit murder in the first place. In determining guilt, criminal cases must show that three factors have come together in the same person: motive, opportunity, and means. Of these three factors, motive is the most important consideration in a criminal trial. But it's also the most important consideration in history. Historians, of course, don't refer to it as *motive*. They like to say that they have figured out *why* history took the course that it did.

Of course, *what* happened is important. Facts are facts, and modern science can do wonders to establish their validity. And you certainly cannot tell a story without cold, hard, irrefutable facts. But when people read history, they don't just want to read about what happened. They also want to know *why* something happened. They want to know the *motive* behind a specific historical event. By crafting a story which explains the real motive for the murder, and verifying both the opportunity and the means, Perry Mason is working as a historian.

Because both the prosecution and Perry Mason are trying to reconstruct the history of a murder, and because doing so requires indentifying the motive for it, they are not just historians. Rather, they are more correctly identified as "psychohistorians." Psychohistory is the application of psychoanalytical principles to understanding causes in history—that is, identifying *motives*.

### When Is a Lawyer Not a Lawyer?

American historian H. Stuart Hughes (1916–1999) in *History as Art and Science: Twin Vistas on the Past* (1964), had a lot to say about discovering the motives behind historical events. For Hughes, applying Freudian psychoanalytical principles to world events would lead to a deeper understanding of history. Knowing the motive behind historical events is crucial for understanding why they occurred, as historical events require *human* agency. People make history. Like Perry Mason, Hughes felt that historians should be careful not to accept the first or easiest explanation for events. He would certainly not have approved of how Lieutenant Tragg and District Attorney Hamilton Burger so quickly arrive at their belief in a suspect's guilt.

Hughes urged historians to be alert to any discrepancy in the facts, and to be alert for a lack of fit of any fact to the whole story. Such discrepancies are warning flags that the whole story is not clearly understood. Even the most trivial fact can turn a story completely around. For example, we see a $500 bonus offered to sublet an already occupied apartment in a building with many comparable units freely available as a clue that forced Perry Mason to completely reconsider what he believed ("The Case of the Crimson Kiss"). Hughes also would have understood why Perry Mason was so successful in arriving at the truth. He urged his fellow historians to have an inner conviction when it comes to approaching history. For Perry Mason, this conviction is that his client is absolutely innocent, regardless of what evidence the district attorney is relying on.

Applying psychoanalytical principles to a collection of historical facts, not accepting the first and typically most obvious explanation for them, being alert to discrepancies in facts, and having an inner conviction when pursuing a line of inquiry into the past, all demonstrate that Perry Mason is an excellent example of the best practices in historical analysis that Hughes believed historians could aspire to. Perry Mason isn't just a defense attorney who specializes in defending people accused of murder. He's clearly a historian—and an excellent one at that. Ladies and gentlemen, the facts demonstrate this conclusion beyond any reasonable doubt!

John V. Karavitis

## Lying on the Witness Stand, and Laying Down the Law

For those of you who are still with me, I have a second conclusion that I would like to establish. At this point, you may very well balk at this claim and stop reading this chapter. Please, bear with me, and raise no objections. As with everything that has come before, I will clearly and plainly support my version of the truth with cold, hard facts.

An interesting thing happens at the end of every episode of Perry Mason. Everyone knows it, and everyone expects it. Typically, in the courtroom, and while on the witness stand, the real murderer is confronted by a set of facts which contradicts his testimony. At this point, the murderer breaks down, confesses, and also provides the motive for the murder. Remember that motive is the most important consideration in a murder trial.

But how can this be? When author Gardner first began to write his novels, and later with the television series of the 1950s/1960s, the *Miranda* case, which established that the accused has to be informed of their right against self-incrimination, unless they voluntarily waive it, hadn't yet been decided. Even so, how foolish could anyone be to admit *in open court* that they had committed a murder? Everyone knows that you remain silent when confronted with an accusation of guilt. I'm not encouraging people to commit murder, now; I'm just saying . . . well . . . you know what I mean! "You're putting words in my mouth! I never said that!" ("The Case of the Sleepwalker's Niece").

You have a right, under the Fifth Amendment, against self-incrimination. And it's the prosecutor's job to prove beyond a reasonable doubt whether you are guilty—you don't have to do their work for them! So, what's going on with Perry Mason typically cornering the real murderer in open court and getting him to break down and confess? Well, remember when I said earlier that a defense attorney isn't just a defense attorney? That he's also, in a sense, a historian? I claim that Perry Mason has another function in the courtroom. And you'll find this assertion even more unbelievable than the first.

Perry Mason is more than just a defense attorney. He is more than a historian. He is also a psychoanalyst.

## When Is a Lawyer Not a Lawyer?

Sigmund Freud (1856–1939) is considered to be the father of psychoanalysis. Psychoanalysis is the set of theories and therapies that are used to explain human mental development, and it provides approaches and tools for curing mental and emotional disturbances. Everyone here understands what I am talking about. We've all seen movies where a psychoanalyst has his patient lie down on a couch in a dimly-lit office, and then either engages in free association of words, or asks the patient to go into excruciating detail about their parents and childhood. These word games are used to get the patient to verbally open up and confront the real cause of his psychological issues, and it's the reason why psychoanalysis is also referred to as "the talking cure."

Although what the psychoanalyst does for his patients can appear to be confusing and unrealistic at best, and comical and futile at worst, the idea behind psychoanalysis can be put rather plainly. The patient is in some form of mental or emotional anguish or distress; and, as a result of this, he creates a type of psychological resistance to the truth. This psychological resistance is referred to as a *defense mechanism*. Denial, displacement, repression, regression, reaction formation, and sublimation are all types of defense mechanisms that an emotionally distressed person can use to block out that part of reality which is the cause of his anguish. The psychoanalyst uses various tools and therapies in order to have his patient talk about and confront what brought about these defense mechanisms. By acknowledging their inner demons, the patient will be able to confront his problems and resolve them.

Someone who has committed murder, unless he is a completely amoral sociopath, will definitely have strong feelings about his criminal act. The rage that led to the murder could either have been impulsive or the result of a long-simmering hatred. Regardless, the murder occurred, and most murders aren't committed by sociopaths. They're committed by people like you and me. Yes, normal people commit murder! (Something to keep in mind . . .)

But murder isn't the normal state of affairs for most people, and, especially with the possibility of discovery and incarceration, or even capital punishment, there would be a great drive to conceal the truth. With the police believing that someone else had committed the murder, it would be easy to just fall into their conveniently erroneous version of the story and "forget" what had actually happened.

In fact, there are many times when we see the real murderer, or an accomplice, be very helpful throughout the course of Perry Mason's investigation. However, as the story of what *really* happened—the *why*, along with the *what*—is determined by Perry Mason, the real murderer is finally forced to openly confront the truth. This invariably occurs in the last few minutes of the preliminary hearing in the court room. Perry Mason draws out a statement from the real murderer that contradicts what had up until then been believed to be the real story. When confronted by both his lie, with which he had sought to repress the truth, and the truth, the real murderer breaks down on the witness stand, and confesses. This is exactly what psychoanalysts work toward—that moment of self-realization called "abreaction," when the patient comes face to face with the repressed truth, and has to look at both it and the lie that has been used to repress it. But is it that knowing the truth sets you free? Free from continuing to live a lie, that is, if nothing else. Or is it that, try as you might, you can never really escape the truth?

Perry Mason is not just a defense attorney. Besides relying in part on psychoanalytical principles to discover the truth, and acting as a historian whose focus is the motive for a murder, he's also a psychoanalyst. (Don't deny it! Face the facts and accept them! You know it's true!)

### The Truth, the Whole Truth, and . . .

Is anyone still reading this chapter? I hope so. Like I said, I didn't quite know what to do when the call for abstracts came out for *Perry Mason and Philosophy*. I mean, I grew up watching the Raymond Burr episodes on my family's black and white Zenith television. I loved this television series. But a philosophical essay about Perry Mason? About *lawyers*? Could I write a chapter about watching paint dry instead?

At times like this, the best thing to do is to simply let the facts speak for themselves, just as Perry Mason would. And

## When Is a Lawyer Not a Lawyer?

I think the conclusions I've arrived at are unique, but also irrefutable. When you see Perry Mason in action, you think "lawyer" and "court room," you don't think "historian," and definitely not "psychoanalyst." But when it comes to determining the motive for what happened, both practices are searching for the truth—for why people behaved as they did. Both practices are also present in the criminal legal system. And as with every episode of *Perry Mason*, I've let the facts speak for themselves.

But this isn't the end of my chapter. I have a final conclusion to present. And if you are a die-hard *Perry Mason* fan, and you didn't particularly care for my first two conclusions, this last one will definitely make you never want to defend *me* in a criminal trial. (Don't worry, I won't take it personally. You have a right to your own opinion—to your own version of the truth.)

Perry Mason is an interesting character. I don't know if his creator, Erle Stanley Gardner, created such a one-dimensional character on purpose, or if that was simply the style for that type of detective and pulp fiction back in the 1930s. But hasn't it ever struck you as strange that we never see Perry Mason have a private life? There are many times when he has lunch and dinner with Paul Drake and Della Street. But these are meals with business associates and co-workers, not people whom he knows outside of the workplace.

When Perry Mason is seen participating in some kind of extracurricular activity or time off, it's typically either in the presence of Paul Drake, or he's completely alone. We see him on a late-night fishing trip with Paul Drake ("The Case of the Negligent Nymph"). We see him spending time in a remote cabin during a local water carnival—alone ("The Case of the Angry Mourner"). He does go on a hunting trip with an old friend. But not that close of a friend, as Perry Mason admits to never having met one of the sheriff's daughters: "This is the first time I've seen Charlotte" ("The Case of the Violent Village"). Without fail, even in these moments away from his work, Perry Mason invariably gets dragged into yet another murder case. I know that showing details of his private life would probably interfere with the economy of a fifty-three-minute television episode. But still, something from his private life should have crept into the television screenplays, at least on occasion over 271 episodes spanning nine consecutive television seasons.

Yet we see nothing.

And perhaps we see nothing because there is nothing. Because outside of working long hours at his office, visiting clients, conducting investigations on his own, presenting his cases in open court, and sharing a meal with business associates and co-workers, perhaps there really is nothing more to Perry Mason. Even his relationship with his confidential secretary, Della Street, which could have led to an amorous situation, remains forever professional yet cordial. Although the look on Della's face as she gives Perry a neck massage late one evening in the office is very suggestive, the look on Perry's face shows us that he is distracted, lost in the forest of his own thoughts ("The Case of the Sleepwalker's Niece"). And this kind of unbalanced life raises question marks of its own.

When someone focuses exclusively on one thing, they are either suffering from some kind of mental disorder, such as obsessive-compulsive personality, or they are repressing emotional distress by directing their attention toward a positive goal. The psychoanalytical term for this latter behavior is sublimation. Sublimation is the defense mechanism where an individual's socially unacceptable drives are translated into socially acceptable behaviors. As H. Stuart Hughes observed, when you perceive external threats, something as simple as ritual can give you comfort. Ritualistic behavior can help a person deal with anxiety. And isn't taking on a murder case and fighting to get to the truth itself a form of long, drawn-out ritualistic behavior? Especially if that's all you do?

Haven't you also ever wondered how Perry Mason chooses the cases he works on? At times it's a complete mystery. For example, why would a defense attorney who specializes in murder ever bother taking cases dealing with probate ("The Case of the Sulky Girl"), or railroad stock mergers? ("The Case of the Silent Partner"). Why would a defense lawyer agree to interfere with housing development investors in order to help a woman win back her cheating husband? ("The Case of the Nervous Accomplice").

Practicing law requires an attorney to specialize in one particular area. It's simply not possible for any one attorney

## When Is a Lawyer Not a Lawyer?

to be effective in all areas of the law. Perry Mason continues to pursue a case even after acknowledging that no one can win one which involves a cop killing, and with Paul Drake urging him to drop it. In the same episode, Lieutenant Tragg sternly warns Perry Mason. "As a lawyer, you're supposed to know better" ("The Case of the Moth-Eaten Mink"). Perry Mason's specialty is clearly stated by Della Street. "It's your own fault. You shouldn't be fooling around with wills and sulky heiresses anyway. Your specialty is murder" ("The Case of the Sulky Girl").

And, at a time when, in the state of California, a first-degree murder conviction would have meant a one-way trip to the gas chamber, what could be more socially acceptable than defending people from an erroneous charge of murder? What could his inner demon be? If he could focus his piercing, relentless intellect on his own life, what would he discover?

What drives Perry Mason? What is he hiding?

# 12
# What about Della Street?

NOELL BIRONDO

Della Street is an excellent legal secretary—she's dedicated and diligent and dependably fulfills her obligations as a secretary. She's also a 'team player'—she makes essential contributions to the office that go well beyond her obligations as a secretary.

Della Street works for Perry Mason, the famous defense attorney, who runs his own one-man law office. By that I mean he's the only lawyer in the office, but he's also the only man. He is the boss, *el jefe*, 'the Chief.' And while I've got nothing against Gertie, the receptionist, when it comes to Della Street you have to admit, she works hard for the money. By the time she's trailing suspects after hours and working the case with her boss well past midnight, she's gone pretty far beyond a standard nine-to-five. Why does Della do this?

Is her dedicated behavior genuinely admirable—or is it actually something regrettable, and even sort of sad? These are questions about Della Street's motivations for doing what she does, questions about her *reasons* for doing them. Such questions fall into the area of philosophy known as 'moral psychology', which is a subsection of moral philosophy or ethics. A person's reasons for doing what she does are connected to her character—to the kind of person she is overall.

We might, for instance, ask the following questions. Is Della Street committed to justice for the sake of the clients themselves? Does she want to help *them*? That would show she's compassionate and benevolent, that she wants to help people. Or does she think that Perry Mason's defense of his clients serves the greater good? Does she think it's good for society *as a whole*? Or does she act on behalf of a judicial system that ensures fairness and law and order? That would show that she's concerned about justice itself and doing one's moral duty.

## Della's Multiple Motivations

Alternatively, maybe Della acts for more personal reasons. Maybe she befriends suspects and manipulates evidence (or plans to do so)—sometimes on the verge of sacrificing her integrity—to serve the interests of Perry Mason, her boss. Isn't that what it means to be called a 'team player'— that you're willing to sacrifice your integrity in order to get the job done? So maybe she's 'just doing her job'. She does what's in the best interest of the office, something that's also in her own interest. Does that make Della Street self-centered—or even selfish? Actually, doesn't it seem as if Della would welcome a romance with Perry Mason? Isn't that one of her reasons for working so hard? Would that mean that Della Street is romantically sort of naive? Wouldn't that show that Della Street is sort of gullible?

By the time we ask those questions—especially if we dislike their tone—some new and different questions begin to pop up. They take on a darker tone. Is Della Street being taken advantage of by Perry Mason, as any lower-level employee can be by expectations that go well beyond their professional obligations? Isn't her portrayal as a 'team player' itself the result of mid-century sexism? Why does she have to work so hard for the money anyway, for the modest wages she presumably makes as a secretary in a tiny law office?

Shouldn't she be given a promotion by now (or at least a huge pay increase) for constantly putting in all those long hours? Indeed, given how much Della Street knows about the law, why doesn't Perry Mason pay for her to go to law school? That would double the legal capacity in his office. Even for a very small practice that would seem to be a good investment. So let's spend some time asking questions directed toward Perry Mason—as the just and courageous legal advocate he is. What about Della Street?

*What about Della Street?*

## What's a Girl to Do?

As I said, Della Street is an excellent legal secretary. But what does it mean to say something like that? According to one way of understanding this type of evaluation—an evaluation of Della Street *as* a secretary—it means she exhibits all of the appropriate traits, all of the skills and abilities, that any reasonable person would expect a good secretary to exhibit. Today we'd point to the data processing and organizational skills expected of administrative assistants. But well before computers and smartphones, a secretary's having excellent typing skills and the ability to take notes in hyper-efficient Gregg shorthand, would top any list. Indeed, I have it on excellent authority that the ability to take notes in Gregg shorthand can often, even today, get you an interview with even the most elevated corporate executives—presidents of major banks and partners at Big Four accounting firms—which is admittedly not Della's line, but still.

Della Street's use of shorthand becomes crucial in unexpected ways. She uses shorthand in the office for taking notes about what clients say or what Perry Mason says—for instance when instructing her on how to edit legal briefs. But consider what happens outside of the office, and well after hours, in the *Case of the Lonely Heiress* (1948—not the television episode of the same title; I've chosen this book at random for purposes of illustration). In this case, Della proposes the risky but high-reward plan of returning to the murder scene to 'rearrange', let's say, the crime scene evidence previously examined by Lieutenant Tragg—a real piece of 'skullduggery' as Perry and Della refer to it.

The scene is the apartment of the victim. The main murder suspect is Perry Mason's client, Marilyn Marlowe—the lonely heiress of the book's title. But Perry and Della suspect a different woman, a certain Mrs. Caddo. (In the end they're all wrong, and Perry Mason is the first to sort out who the real killer is.) When Perry and Della are on their way *out* of the apartment of the victim—this is around 1:30 a.m.—they're confronted by a police officer and, somewhat surprisingly, an accusatory Mr. Robert Caddo. The way they get out of this jam is ingenious. Perry Mason convinces the officer that the two of them were actually trying to get *into* this apartment—and that Caddo never saw them go into the apartment as Caddo insists that he had. Perry Mason first wants to get clear on Caddo's story, so that he can poke holes in it. Notice Della's role in how this happens:

> "The minute you saw us coming up here to this door," Mason said, his foot touching Della Street's toe, "you went dashing off to the nearest telephone."
> "I've already told you that," Caddo said.
> "You certainly have," Mason said. "I want you to get the significance of that, officer. The minute he saw us come up here on the porch, he dashed to the telephone."
> "Because I knew what you were trying to do. I knew you were trying to get in there and plant some evidence on my wife. I'd had a suspicion all along that you'd do something like that. You . . . Hey, officer, that woman is taking this stuff down in shorthand."
> "Sure she is," Mason said.
> The officer turned. Della Street, standing back in the corner, had taken a shorthand notebook and fountain pen from her pocket and her hand was flying over the page, making dashes and pothooks.

You can see where this is going: It's not long before Caddo contradicts himself, as shown by Della's record of what he said. Della Street's excellent secretarial skills are a luxury for Perry Mason to have even in the middle of the night—where he might find himself cross-examining, before an officer of the law, the doorstep testimony of a hostile witness.

This point about role-specific traits or abilities—the traits or abilities that go hand-in-hand with certain social and professional roles—is obviously not limited to the traditional role of secretaries. We all make assumptions about the traits we expect from good parents or police officers or optometrists or friends. Our assumptions about the appropriate traits for different roles allow us to make evaluations of people in these roles—about how someone is both a good optometrist, for instance, and also a good mother. These assumptions also allow for evaluations that go the other way, for negative evaluations of people's behavior, when they fail to exhibit the traits appropriate to a certain role.

Someone might be a poor office administrator because she obstructs, rather than facilitates, the professional activities

## What about Della Street?

of her office. She might make travel reimbursements more difficult than they need to be—either from negligence or personal animosity or a kind of professional resentment. Alternatively, a police officer might apply legal criteria differently across different racial groups—in violation of his professional obligation to administer the law impartially—thereby showing himself to be at fault in this respect.

Della Street doesn't display any such failures in her role as legal secretary, and in fact she often volunteers—well beyond her professional obligations—to contribute a perspective that Perry Mason, and Paul Drake, the private investigator, do not naturally inhabit. This is what might be called a 'woman's perspective' on the motivations of suspects or various aspects of the case. The idea that there *is* such a thing as a 'woman's perspective' was familiar to Gardner's generation, and to my mother's and grandmothers' generations, and the idea is still discussed today by leading feminist philosophers. One of Della Street's contributions to the office—as both Perry Mason and Paul Drake appreciate—is her take on the available evidence from a "woman's angle" (as she herself puts it).

## I'm a Wildcat When I Get Started

In some of the most influential ancient traditions in philosophy, spanning multiple continents, our ethical behavior as a whole can be gauged by how we measure up as people *as a whole*—by whether we exhibit, as the human beings we are, the appropriate traits of character and intellect that good human beings ought to exhibit.

The Western tradition traces its lineage to ancient Greece, to the philosophers who lived and taught there, for instance the immeasurably influential philosophy of Aristotle (384–322 B.C.E.)—his teacher being one of the greatest all-time teachers of philosophy, the immeasurably influential Plato (around 429–347 B.C.E.). Some excellent traits of character—at the top of almost any list—are honesty, courage, kindness, generosity, and justice. These are traits of character that most people try to instill in their children and cultivate in themselves. They are exemplary traits of character.

One especially important trait is the trait of 'practical wisdom' or 'practical intelligence.' This is a trait that enables good people, in their deliberations about what to do, to make morally admirable decisions. Perry Mason exhibits this type of practical intelligence in a 'role-specific' way when he deliberates about, and decides upon, the best way to investigate and prosecute a case. Indeed, he's justly famous for the practical intelligence he exhibits as a defense attorney, in versatile and ever-ingenious ways.

But Perry Mason also shows a blind spot in his exercise of practical intelligence *as a person*, because he tends to overlook (or at least to leave under-acknowledged) the contributions made by Della Street. This is a failure of recognition or appreciation. Like most of us, Perry Mason could do better at giving credit where credit is due. This is a flaw that most of us display some of the time, and some of us display most of the time—not only toward our co-workers, but also toward our spouses, our parents, our children, and our friends. It's a place where most of us could be doing better.

But Perry Mason knows that none of us is perfect, and he rightly stresses the importance of moral character in living a good human life. We learn later about Mrs. Caddo's extreme—and even violent—reactions to her husband's suspected infidelities. She confronts the suspected paramour at her workplace or her home. She throws a fiery tantrum, and she throws real physical objects. As Mrs. Caddo puts it herself with evident pride, "I'm a wildcat when I get started." Mrs. Caddo also turns up at Perry Mason's office, clearly on a warpath. She's prepared to raise hell over Perry Mason's involvement with her husband's romances, for his introducing her husband to Marilyn Marlowe, that "snaky-hipped brunette." (Perry Mason has nothing to do with Mr. Robert Caddo's "off the reservation" liaisons with Ms. Marlowe.) Perry Mason's response displays important insights about ethical character. He first remarks sharply on Mr. Caddo's egregious defects of character regarding truthfulness. He tells the aggrieved woman:

> Mrs. Caddo, none of us is perfect. We all of us have our little faults. These are imperfections in character which range from the trivial

### What about Della Street?

to the serious, and none of us is free from them, but in addition to what other minor imperfections he may have, your husband is a liar and I would appreciate it if you'd tell him I said so.

Perry Mason also appreciates a crucial feature about character that Aristotle stressed long ago in his writings on moral philosophy. He appreciates that making a *habit* of bad behavior can easily harden into a general defect of character. Such ethically deficient traits make us—in general and in oh-so-predictable ways—unappreciative, or impatient, or spineless, or greedy, or needy, or cruel. That's the dark side of this truth about moral habituation, that bad behavior can do damage to our characters. Perry Mason even emphasizes this point. Turning to Mrs. Caddo's own bad behavior, he asks her:

> "Do you think that being a wildcat, as you term it, buys you anything?"
> Mrs. Caddo sank down in the big client's chair and grinned at Perry Mason. "I know very well that it does. That's the way to handle Bob."
> "Of course," Mason said, "all of these tirades, these fits of temper, gradually leave an indelible mark upon your character."
> "Oh, I suppose so," she said wearily, "but just between you and me and the guidepost, Mr. Mason, I go through these tantrums just to protect my vested interests. They aren't fits of temper. They're an act."

That's what she tells herself, anyway. If her temper tantrums really are just an act then maybe they won't negatively affect her character. But it sort of seems like she's kidding herself.

On the brighter side, making a habit of *good* behavior can be the first step toward cultivating admirable, or even ethically excellent traits of character. Such ethically excellent traits make us grateful, and patient, and courageous, and sharing, and caring. This is why we remind young children to say "Thank you" in response to acts of kindness. At the very beginning, and for a good while afterwards, they're just mouthing words. But once the child begins to see the point of this phrase, and to understand and embrace the practice of expressing gratitude, then a crucial transition begins to take place. Those very same words have now become—at least when she says them sincerely—genuine expressions of gratitude.

They're no longer just words.

If all goes well, she'll go on to exhibit the *character trait* of gratitude or gratefulness—a stable and ethically excellent trait of character. She will have become a grateful person. She has become an excellent human being in this respect, just as Della Street is an excellent secretary in so many professional respects. In each of the two cases, the excellent character traits contribute to, or even constitute, a greater whole—being an excellent human being and being an excellent secretary—and this is no accident. It's no accident that the ability to keep tempo, for instance, is an excellent trait for a musician, or that patience is an excellent trait for a teacher.

## The 'Feminine Charms' of Employees

Although Perry Mason displays a single-minded commitment to justice when it comes to his clients, his relationship with Della Street is more problematic. Della Street often makes indispensable contributions to Perry Mason's success—by ingratiating herself to witnesses, or working long after business hours have ended, in order to obtain crucial information about the case in question. But Della Street is still, after all, his secretary. Investigating the crime and its suspects is the obligation of Paul Drake, the private investigator, not the obligation of a legal secretary!

Has Erle Stanley Gardner, in fact, in creating the character of Della Street, merely created a romantic doormat for his hero? Consider this episode as one piece of evidence. When Della proposes the risky plan discussed earlier, to revisit the crime scene and rearrange the evidence in their favor, Perry Mason is exuberant. Here is how he expresses it:

> Mason got to his feet, took Della Street into his arms and kissed her. She laughed up at him, and he said, "Why is it your feminine charms are never so alluring as when you've thought of some piece of skullduggery?"
>
> "It's a subject we can discuss later," she said. "Right now we have work to do. Suppose Tragg's having the place watched?"

### What about Della Street?

"That's what we'll have to find out."
"And if we get caught?"
"We're just there looking for evidence—and if Tragg doesn't believe that, your feminine charms will have to go to work again," Mason replied.
"On Tragg? Let's not get caught," Della Street said.

Today this episode, which takes place in Della Street's home after midnight, would presumably be a slam-dunk case of sexual harassment. True, Perry Mason might not have to settle the case for $20 million as in the high-profile sexual harassment cases of today. And it's true that Della Street seems willing to go along with these mid-century professional antics. But even so, Perry Mason is her boss. Does that mean Perry Mason is committed to justice in his role as defense attorney, but not to justice in his role as employer, or in his 'personal life'?

Doesn't Perry Mason display his own imperfections of character here (and not such small imperfections either) in his relationship with Della Street, his secretary? Isn't it true that while Perry Mason is courageous in court, he's sort of timid (or worse) when it comes to his romantic relationships? Is the case of Perry Mason, then, the case of the romantic coward? Or do his past traumas somehow also matter?

These are questions that moral philosophy can help us to answer—and even to see clearly enough to know how to ask, especially when no one else seems fazed by the morally problematic behavior of our heroes and others around us.[1]

---

[1] My thanks and dedication to Elizabeth Signorelli (born Stringer), life-long *Perry Mason* fan and retired executive assistant, mother and friend.

# IV

## Story

# 13
# Perry Mason as Greek Tragedy

JANET MCCRACKEN

We'd all agree that the *Perry Mason* show is formulaic: Person A, designated as "good" or at least "innocent" by virtue of seeking Mason's help, is defended against a murder charge, and during the trial (usually) Person B, under Perry's skillful examination, confesses to the murder.

Sometimes we feel sorry for Person B, sometimes we feel righteously indignant; regardless, once B has confessed to the crime. A is often out of the picture, and the episode moves quickly to a lighthearted epilogue. The Greek philosopher Aristotle discovered the secret of this formula almost 2,500 years ago, and described it in his *Poetics*, where he claimed that a successful tragedy helped the audience build up and then, at the climax, release, feelings of pity and fear.

Drama has to involve you, and then *release* you. Aristotle believed that drama is therapeutic—not just in the sense that it feels good to let out these emotions (although that's important)—but also because it makes us better people to learn how these emotions work. And for Aristotle, as for Mason, drama is ultimately all about justice.

Consider, for instance, "The Case of the Silent Partner" from Season One (one of my favorites). Perry's client is Mildred Kimber, the meek, plain-looking owner of a successful orchid nursery. She is charged with the murder of the gambler, Sam Lynk, who won her husband's stock certificates in a rigged poker game.

Before the murder, Lola Florey, the platinum blonde, savvy, hostess at the casino, witnessed Lynk cheating, and teamed up with Mrs. Kimber to expose the fraud to Mason. But Lola is non-fatally poisoned before she can make the appointment, the same night Lynk is killed. Shortly after Lola returns from the hospital, her home is burned down. The case never even gets to the courtroom: Perry is at the scene with Lieutenant Tragg immediately, having figured out that Lola is the murderer, and that she has poisoned herself, and even set fire to her own apartment, to shift suspicion away from herself. The confession scene is wonderfully operatic; noir; tragic: Lola sits among the burnt wreckage, wearing Della's coat over her negligée, admiring Mason for his intelligence, and facing the consequences of her crime with a slick nobility, saying "Sure, Lieutenant; I would have had to find a new place to live anyway."

In the epilogue, no mention is made whatever of the Kimbers, although Tragg mentions the stock certificates. Instead, the discussion is all about Lola; Della refers to her as a "lady" and she and Perry agree that they liked her. Tragg brings them a present from Lola—a box of the kind of chocolates she poisoned herself with—and the three of them chuckle about their reluctance to try a piece.

Notice that we don't know Lola's motive, and we don't care. We've been told that she's in love with Lynk, but we've been given no indication that Lynk was cheating on her. This ending to "The Case of the Silent Partner" puts the *Mason* theme in high relief. We don't really care that Mrs. Kimber's case was dismissed, and however much we may have wondered whodunit, we could never really have guessed that Lola was the murderer—we are offered nowhere near enough clues to pick her out among the several suspects. That's because neither exonerating the accused nor guessing the identity of the murderer is required to achieve the hypnotic dramatic effect of a good *Perry Mason* episode. Neither of these is required to feel that justice has been done when the credits roll.

## What Makes a Good Tragedy

According to Aristotle, a good tragedy—one whose outcome we experience as just or fair—need not pose a puzzle for us to figure out, nor actually depict courtroom justice being served. A good tragedy need only depict *misfortune*, something fearworthy or pitiful, and allow us to release those feelings somehow. Its most powerful, most artful, elements are not seeing the innocent defendant acquitted, but rather *reversals of fortune* and *"discoveries,"* or *revelations* of knowledge. In other words, to make a good tragedy, the misfortune should happen to someone previously in a good situation, and be revealed to the audience as new knowledge. If something bad happens or threatens to happen to an upstanding person, and if we learn something at the climax of the tragedy that corrects that unjust situation, it doesn't matter whether the two elements have anything to do with one another.

In simple tragedies, according to Aristotle, the hero suffers a misfortune. Some simple tragedies are terrifically enjoyable, like the *Die Hard* movies. But let's face it, all that happens in those movies is that Bruce Willis survives two straight hours of getting beaten up. For Aristotle, a great tragedian wove a more complicated plot, and Aristotle identified two crucial ways plots can be complex. The first way to complicate a plot is to include a *reversal of fortune*. In other words, the misfortune that occurs in the story is much more effective if the character who suffers it starts out with a good life. Two-hour death scenes, as in *Terms of Endearment* or *Dead Man Walking* never fail to use up the Kleenexes. But because they never fail, they're sort of an easy way out for the producers. When, on the other hand, the great hero Oedipus (in Aristotle's favorite play, by Sophocles) who saved his city from the plague by solving the riddle of the Sphinx—when Oedipus turns out to have sinned very badly and pokes out his own eyes at the end of the play—that takes us to a whole new level of complexity and thoughtfulness. Think: *Million Dollar Baby, Stella Dallas, Old Yeller, Saving Private Ryan*.

## Climax and Discovery

The second way to complicate a plot, according to Aristotle, is to pin the climax on a *discovery*, the revelation of some kind of knowledge. Again, *Oedipus* fits the bill perfectly. And in recognizing how effective discovery is to a dramatic plot, Aristotle essentially foretold the popularity of murder mysteries and detective stories. Any such story monopolizes on Aristotle's notion of discovery. Now, most murder mysteries or detective stories give the readers or the audience well-hidden clues—among the red herrings—as to the identity of the culprit. This makes the audience try to second-guess the story, making it into something of a game for them, a competition with the detective.

There's nothing wrong with that: it follows the Sherlock Holmes model, and continually entertains audiences. But as Aristotle and Erle Stanley Gardner both knew, it's not at all necessary. The drama works in a complicated, clever way as long as the hero and the audience discover something, regardless of whether they could have figured it out on their own. That's why we're rarely given enough clues to beat Perry to the punch. In fact, Perry's identification of the murderer often surprises Paul, whom we know is a great detective.

Sometimes Perry plays a kind of magical hunch, sometimes he lays a trap to catch one of several possible suspects, sometimes he seems to have an epiphany while he's questioning someone on the witness stand. But more often than not, we rely completely on Perry to reveal the guilty party; we could not guess her identity in a million years. Hence, the requisite close-up reaction shots of all the suspects sitting in the courtroom during Perry's examinations. The producers are rubbing it in our faces: no matter what the person on the witness stand is saying right now, *you don't know who the murderer is*!

## Always the Confession

The point is, we never just find out whodunit in a *Perry Mason* episode, and we usually can't even deduce it. Instead, the secret of the *Perry Mason* formula is the *confession*. Regardless of the specifics of the case, no *Perry Mason* murderer is ever caught and arrested and dragged away in handcuffs, still proclaiming their innocence. No *Perry Mason* murderer ever gets away with their crime, and no *Perry Mason* murderer ever denies their guilt, once caught. *Every Perry Mason* murderer admits to their crime. Sometimes this admission consists merely of a pitiful look downward, like Mr. Hays in "The Case of the Pint-Sized Client" (Season Two), after Perry asks him how it feels to have committed robbery and murder for nothing; sometimes the murderer just looks up at Paul, obviously caught and surrendering, like Jim Ferris (William Campbell), who faked his own death and fled to Mexico in "The Case of the Ill-Fated Faker" (Season Four). Sometimes the murderer makes a smart crack, as in "The Case of the Wandering Widow" (Season Four), in which Morgan Riley, pardoned after serving several years in prison for an earlier murder when new evidence is brought out, turns out to have committed both the earlier murder and the one for which Mason's client is accused. "I got away with it last time," he smirks from the witness stand, "Maybe I should have quit while I was ahead." Sometimes we are graced with a good yarn from the murderer, a long backstory—one we could never have guessed—that accounts for the murderer's actions, such as in "The Case of the Roving River" in Season Five, when Seth Tyson confesses at length to a decades-old murder that necessitated the murder for which Mason's client is accused.

In one wonderful episode in Season Three, "The Case of the Wayward Wife," we don't know how the trial turned out: Arthur Poe (Marshall Thompson), a former POW and a great literary talent, returned home to find that his scheming cellmate Ben Sutton, the murder victim, had left Poe for dead trying to escape from their Chinese captors and published Poe's prison diary under his—Sutton's—name, making lots of money and garnering wide critical acclaim. Sutton's wife was accused of the crime. We leave the courtroom when a third cellmate, Wilson, repeatedly and heatedly denies having killed Sutton. After the hearing has concluded—we as yet don't know the outcome—Perry goes to visit Poe in the VA Hospital, where, now near death, Poe confesses to the crime. Leaving Poe's room, Perry tells Tragg, "You know it *was* self-defense." The episode ends as Tragg quietly closes the door, leaving Poe in peace. We never hear another thing about the defendant.

The genius of *Perry Mason* is that we always see the guilty party admit to his crime, so that we really feel the satisfaction of justice being done. Were the murderer, say, killed in a police shootout, we might be relieved that he was no longer a threat to the community, or happy that our hero won the day or, more often, aggravated at the current state of society. In such cases, often associated with perfectly good police procedurals like *Hawaii Five-O*, *Kojak*, or *NYPD Blue*, gritty realism does the dramatic work, leaving the audience always on the side of the returning hero whose heart, stamina, and dedication to an ugly job make him an admirable person. Similarly, in regular detective dramas, whether very good ones like *The Rockford Files*, or more workaday ones like *Murder, She Wrote*, we find out who committed the crime, and we're relieved to know it. But our sympathies start with the detective hero and end with the detective hero, while the murderer may well be captured, killed or stand trial—even perhaps be acquitted—long after the end of the episode. In those shows, to be sure, Aristotle still had his finger on the pulse: we still build up pity and fear, and still release these feelings. And we still learn about justice. But in those kinds of shows, we side with the hero who, since we know he'll return in the next episode, seems almost superhuman in his good qualities. According to Aristotle, this diminishes our ability to identify with the hero, however, and so makes our lesson about justice more superficial than in *Perry Mason*, where we see the murderer realize the true consequences of his action, sometimes at length.

Aristotle could have told Erle Stanley Gardner and *Mason's* producers—Ben Brady, Gail Patrick Jackson, and Sam White—that audiences would happily watch and rewatch *Perry Mason* well into the next century. According to Aristotle, a good tragedy relies first and foremost on its *plot*. And the plot of a good tragedy has to have a beginning, a middle, and an *end*. This may sound obvious, but consider how many TV dramas, especially today, develop plot arcs for multiple-season binge-watching and then are canceled before they get to finish the whole arc, or have to end things more quickly than they might have wanted, like the wonderful show *Freaks and Geeks*, or the greatly-missed *Firefly*; or how many TV shows with multi-episode arcs got off to a great start in the first season or two but then couldn't sustain their dramatic tension, like *Twin Peaks* or *Lost*.

We begin to appreciate the genius required to introduce a whole set of characters, bring the story to a dramatic climax, and then wrap it all up in a neat bow and release the audience completely, in one hour.

Perry Mason *as Greek Tragedy*

## Stick to the Formula

Part of the greatness of *Perry Mason* is that there are no cliffhangers: we never wonder what's going to happen in the next episode, never worry about whether Della is going to get fed up and leave her job, or fall in love with someone else and get married; we never worry that Paul is really going to lose his license. We leave every episode completely satisfied and ready to go on with our lives. And while it takes genius to achieve this, one quality of that genius is never to tire of the formula: the successful end of a *Perry Mason* episode is *always* achieved by the on-screen confession and the lighthearted epilogue which follows it immediately after the commercial break.

In "The Case of the Screaming Woman" (Season One), a vile gossip columnist, Mary Kay Davis, attempts to buy a baby in order to hold onto her husband, a powerful politician. When the goodhearted doctor who has made a career of adopting out the babies of unwed mothers refuses Mary Kay's request, she steals his record book and attempts to blackmail a baby out of him. Any number of people hate Mary Kay: the doctor, his nurse (who is actually accused of the crime), her husband, her husband's mistress, her secretary, her secretary's boyfriend (one of the good doctor's adoptees, who is named in the list), and her attorney, who would like to get in on the blackmail deal. Other than the fact that she has been, perhaps, the most emotional of the group, there would be no way to guess that the secretary, Miss Cooper is the murderer. Perry doesn't know: he resorts to hiring a voice actress to impersonate Mary Kay on a fake Dictaphone cylinder, pretending to be about to name the adoptees on the list. Only then does Miss Cooper, sobbing, admit to the crime.

## Good and Bad Characters

The second most important element of a tragedy, according to Aristotle, is the *characters*. We can't feel pity or fear without *characterization*: this is what makes every good tragedy a lesson in justice. First, we must be able to relate to the hero of a tragedy, Aristotle claimed: in other words, we have to be able to imagine ourselves in his or her place. So the hero has to be, morally, pretty much like the audience members—well-intentioned, basically good, but flawed. It's tragic when William Wallace gets disemboweled in *Braveheart*, because he's a noble, historical (or at least believable) character. If the hero is a little worse than the audience members—say, he's really short, like Buster Keaton or Joe Pesci, really nerdy and arrogant, like Sheldon Cooper in *The Big Bang Theory*, or really superficial, like the quartet in *Seinfeld*—then when the hero suffers misfortune, as is requisite for any plot, it'll be comedic. It's comical when Kramer destroys his complexion by smoking in *Seinfeld*, because he's a (very believable) hipster doofus.

If the characters are *very* much worse than us, however, we cheer at their misfortune: it's victorious when Dennis Hopper's character (Howard Payne) gets his head knocked off by a subway lamp in *Speed* (1994), because he's a messed-up, evil, ex-policeman. Similarly, we cheer when a character *very* much better than us survives a perilous situation: it's victorious when John McClane walks out of the Nakatomi Plaza in *Die Hard* (1988) because he's superhumanly beaten up, but still alive.

We feel pity and fear for the misfortunes of good people, and laugh at the misfortunes of (slightly) bad people, because it's what they *deserve*. They're not evil, not the villains of the piece; in that case it would strike us as just to see them suffer much worse fates, like death. We don't identify, Aristotle would claim, with really evil characters, and so we feel exultant when they suffer the terrible things they deserve. To make the story a tragedy, claimed Aristotle, just make the hero a little better, morally, than the members of the audience. Again, we can't identify with a superhero (or, as Aristotle puts it, with a Greek god), because he has no human frailties: we cheer when a superhero gets out of the inevitable jam that brings the dramatic tension to the story. But in a tragedy, we cry when the hero gets into the jam in the first place.

We weep when Romeo and Juliet, beautiful young people with their lives ahead of them, trying to unite their feuding families, commit double suicide. We sob when we discover that Duke has been telling the story of their love to an Alzheimer's-ridden Allie who doesn't recognize him in *The

## Perry Mason as Greek Tragedy

*Notebook.* We lose it when the stoical, dutiful Ennis finds his late beloved Jack's shirt in the closet of his childhood home in *Brokeback Mountain*. To make a tragedy, misfortune must befall a sympathetic, realistic person, whom we nonetheless for some good reason, admire. In that case only, their misfortune is *undeserved*, and we get an opportunity to learn how a good person faces heart-wrenching circumstances. Character, Aristotle claimed, reveals the moral purpose of the agents.

We tend to find examples of tragedy, however, only in movies or plays, not in TV shows, because TV shows are episodic. Since we know the main characters will return in the next episode (unless you include shockers like *Game of Thrones*), it's very hard to make the stakes high enough in a TV show to evoke that sense of undeserved misfortune requisite for a good tragedy. That's why, Aristotle thought, the great Greek tragedies always depicted the mythic heroes and their families—because if the audience already knows the main characters and their stories, the author doesn't have to spend a lot of time developing the characters, and can get right down to the business of building up pity or fear. And that's why TV series can't usually release the pity or fear, because their characters, once established, can't undergo the kind of misfortune that would be necessary to make us cry or scream.

But *Perry Mason*, by cleverly fitting the Aristotelian formula into an episodic format, succeeds where others fail. It manages this feat by keeping all the recurring characters *out of the story*. In only two episodes are any of the main characters actually embroiled in the case: "Paul Drake's Dilemma" (Season Three, in which Paul, in self-defense, punches the murder victim and is knocked out when he falls from the retaliatory punch, minutes before the murder), and the very late "The Case of the Dead Ringer" (Season Nine)—my least favorite episode for precisely this reason, in which Raymond Burr plays a dual role, Perry and Mr. Grimes, an old sailor, used by opposing council to discredit Perry.

Otherwise, Perry, Paul, and Della and all the other regulars, essentially play *hosts* to the characters who actually have skin in the game. These characters, played by an enormous list of terrific guest stars, are developed very quickly as likeable, unlikeable, hateful, cool, beautiful, clever, or wild. Thus, the audience can be sad or afraid for the accused, develop feelings about the various suspects, and respond to the dénouement—the confession—in the course of a single hour without ever worrying about the main characters. It's ingenious.

So what's most amazing about *Perry Mason* is the efficiency with which it creates character and manipulates our sympathies, so that we begin sympathetic with the accused, and yet can be released from the drama by catharting our pity or fear *through the murderer*'s confession. The clever trick is the staunch dedication to the formula, which disallows the main characters from getting involved in any of the cases. And thus, the show accommodates a nearly infinite variety of characterizations along Aristotle's ethical spectrum, sometimes releasing us with an expression of profound pity, or eerie fear. And most stunning is that the show is able to switch our sympathies however necessary in order to get the right effect from the confession.

## A Cheerful Coda

Once Mason has gotten his confession, the audience must be released. Hence the absolutely ubiquitous lighthearted epilogue, or coda. It's shocking, when you think about it, how quickly Perry, Paul, and Della turn around from a dire or chilling situation to some joke about, say, how Paul's upcoming date has fallen through, or how Della is hungry and wants a steak dinner. Often enough, the epilogue *is* about the accused, with whom we have remained in sympathy. But just as often, we change our sympathies to the murderer, whom we may well have come to admire or like, like Lola in "The Case of the Silent Partner."

In "The Case of the Daring Decoy" (Season One), this change in sympathies is particularly effective. Rose Calvert, the lovely young secretary of oil executive Daniel Conway, and a spy for a rival oilman, is found murdered. Conway, her boss, is accused of the crime. As a part of his investigation, Perry visits the victim's estranged husband Fred Calvert (played to perfection by Jack Weston) before the news is made public, *de facto* notifying Calvert of his wife's death. Calvert initially thinks the attorney is there about obtaining a divorce, and claims that Rose will come to her senses and drop the divorce suit soon. "She has a good thing here," he says. "You see, this house is all paid for; not a cent of mortgage on it."

As usual, many characters in addition to the accused have motives for killing Rose Calvert: the rival oil executive with whom she's been having an affair, the rival oilman's wife, and others. Under Perry's examination at the trial, Daniel Calvert admits initially only that that he'd gone back to the city, to Rose's apartment, to recover a letter from her mailbox: he'd sent her the deed to his house as an enticement for her to return to him. Our hearts sink. Then, faced with possible identification by a witness, and like a little boy who's been caught stealing a candy bar, Calvert states, "I loved my wife; honest I did, Mr. Mason. . . . I thought she'd come to her senses and come back to me. She wouldn't. She was willing to give up everything. Even the house."

"Then you went to that hotel room," says Perry, with deep sympathy for Calvert, "and you killed her." "Yes," says Calvert, looking down at his feet. "Just the way you said it, Mr. Mason, almost exactly the way you said." There's no way we could have guessed that poor, pitiful, Calvert had done the deed. But now that we know, we can barely hold back our tears for him. Conway is utterly out of our thoughts; Perry does not seem like a hero. Instead, our sympathies have moved from the accused to the guilty party, in the face of this heart-wrenching revelation. We see in Calvert, just as Aristotle would have guessed, how wrong things can go when love is unrequited. And, as Aristotle would also have guessed, in Calvert we see ourselves, we confess our own humiliating sins. Unlike Calvert, however, we're redeemed through this realization, by releasing our pent-up pity in a sad pout or even a tear.

Moments later, after the commercial break, we can put it all behind us and move on to wash the dishes: Perry, Della, and Conway are having a drink in a fancy hotel bar. One of Conway's admiring stockholders, Amelia Armitage, stops by the bar to congratulate the exonerated executive (how did she know where they were? Who cares? What's logic in the face of this amazing, emotional hundred-eighty-degree switch?), and she and Conway start their life together as Perry and Della leave the bar . . . and for us, all is right with the world again.

# 14
# "Yes! I Did It!"

ALEXANDER E. HOOKE

>We have the best witness, a confessing defendant.
>
>—*Black's Law Dictionary*

Readers of Erle Stanley Gardner's novel *The Case of the Daring Decoy* learn of the real murderer's identity only upon his attempted escape from the courtroom. Until then defense attorney Perry Mason was facing considerable circumstantial evidence that provided little hope for him and his client.

Everyone with a financial motive or possible opportunity to murder has a ready alibi. Only Mason's client does not. So Mason pulls off a poker tactic in the courtroom by bluffing the murderer into believing Mason has all the goods on him. As the judge calls for a ten-minute recess, the murderer—his wife was the victim—flees the courtroom, only to be captured by the guards in the hallway.

Viewers of "The Case of the Daring Decoy" as presented in the Perry Mason television show reach a different ending. The defense attorney provides the final piece of the puzzle that will acquit his client by requesting the murder victim's husband to testify. The husband is awkward and hesitant, acknowledging that he owns his house outright and hoped his wife would come to her senses by leaving her paramour and return to him. Mason then presents him with potentially incriminating evidence, as his testimony has contradictions and ignores proven facts. The murderer suddenly breaks down. He could not bear the thought that she loved another man and marry him. Bemoaning his fate, weeping and trembling before judge, jury, and a roomful of spectators—as well as millions of television viewers—the guilty man concludes the drama with a confession. Yes, he did it.

The confession is arguably the most enduring and distinct legacy of the Perry Mason television program. While the shows themselves are unevenly faithful to the original novels, they nevertheless capture the tastes and pleasures of the emerging televisions audiences of the 1950s and 1960s. Namely, there is a market for people who enjoy watching another person's confession. The recent spate of talk shows, reality programs, self-help specials, real judges in action—from Oprah and Dr. Phil to Judge Judy and Jerry Springer—testifies to the on-going pleasure human beings have in witnessing the culminating moment of a fellow human confessing their sins, evil motives, and guilt-ridden misdeeds.

In such a light, Perry Mason is a pioneer in the recent history of popular entertainment. The show anticipated ever new audiences with a curious delight in who confesses and why. This is more than a speech act that admits to a crime—it is a dramatic moment in truth. The miscreant must also explain why he or she did the crime, offering the spectators that cynical joy in judging another.

The viewers have also experienced greed, jealousy, revenge, hatred, entrapment, blackmail, and desperation as among the reasons for wanting the death of someone else, but they did not succumb to murder. How they are different from the murderer is central to the spectators' continued interest. Through this link between drama and the moment of truth, Perry Mason highlights the spectacle of confession.

At least three components comprise a confession spectacle. Unlike the solitary confession—made before God, a torturer, or therapist—Perry Mason entices the murderer to address an insatiably curious public. Second, the confession is dramatic, displaying a range of emotions and explanations while inviting the audience to judge the veracity of the confession. Third, the confession is a surprise. Whereas a Perry Mason novel often features over a dozen suspects and interested parties, the television show is limited by the allotted time. Readers have the luxury of going at their own pace in following the finer details of the story, so when they reach the moment of guilt it is derived from the preceding evidence in the novel. Television viewers, on the other hand, have the same fifty-three minutes to experience the entire story, so for them the unexpected and dramatic confession becomes the culminating moment.

The confession spectacle also poses several philosophical concerns. To discern between an instance of self-knowledge and the self-deception of someone's confession is an uncertain task. At the same time, there are expressions of self-knowledge whose dramatic candor seems undeniable. Given that the one confessing has heretofore misled or lied to the police and investigators, a second concern is the basis for any confidence in the truthfulness of the confession itself. Criteria that apply to most evidence fall short when it comes to confessions. With a public confession, the establishment of truth relies on the response of the audience.

The philosopher Michel Foucault is most renowned for his genealogical studies of madness, sexuality, medical clinics, and the modern prison. Foucault also continuously researched the significance and historical dynamics of human beings attempting to tell the truth about themselves. His 1981 lectures at The Catholic University of Louvain, *Wrong-Doing, Truth-Telling*, provide a conceptual lens to examine and appreciate the dramatic appeal of the confession in the Perry Mason stories. This appeal modifies the opening epigraph from Black's Law Dictionary to "the best witness is a confessing one."

## For the Best Evidence

Circumstantial evidence is infallible *if* it is all available. It is the interpretation of the circumstantial evidence which gives it its bad name.

—Erle Stanley Gardner, Foreword to *The Case of the Angry Mourner.*

Erle Stanley Gardner, the creator of Perry Mason, was a successful lawyer before retiring to devote more attention to his fictional and lucrative writing. The forewords to his novels often include a dedication to forensics experts or criminal investigators who are committed to justice by ascertaining the most accurate evidence and its proper interpretation. Their research and conscientious work aims towards the ideal of innocent suspects (such as Mason's clients) being found not guilty while the real murderers are finally identified. A crime, for Gardner, can be likened to a jigsaw puzzle. It's a matter of putting all the pieces together, a task that demands careful analysis and logic.

Too often, however, investigators and prosecutors rely only on their initial instincts about the arrested suspect and filter out the evidence that counters those instincts. For example, in *The Case of the Lucky Loser*, Mason persuades the Judge that his nemesis, District Attorney Hamilton Burger, is unable to account for fingerprints and the whereabouts of witnesses who might actually be the murderers. The flustered Burger charges Mason with his usual courtroom chicanery and legal loopholes. But the judge admonishes Burger to reconsider the evidence. "I think, Mr. District Attorney... most of the logic, as well as all of the equities, are in favor of Perry Mason's position." And that is how the reader learns that Mason's client is again found not guilty.

A viewer of TV's "The Case of the Lucky Loser" finds a different ending. Mason's client, son of a wealthy tycoon, has plenty of motive and opportunity to kill a relative in the family. Instead, Mason shows to the courtroom and television audience that the victim was killed by his own wife. She was having an affair with the tycoon's lawyer and wanted to stay with him forever. Their scheme almost worked. Once Mason finally convinces his client to realize that his wife has been a traitor, the attorney is able to present insurmountable evidence to elicit the shrieks of confession from the real murderer, sitting among courtroom spectators. Only then does the viewer realize that Mason's client is not guilty.

These contrasting experiences are less about the on-going disputes over translating literature into a visual medium than about the relation between the story and the audience. Readers of a Perry Mason novel can take several days to enjoy the 150–250 page story unfolding at their own pace. If part of their enjoyment is rereading passages that might reveal subtle clues for facts which eventually help Mason to

## "Yes! I Did It!"

identify the real murderer, the book version allows them that freedom and extended focus on the plot's subtleties.

The televised version does not have that luxury. It compels the viewer to keep focus for a single 52–53 minute program, without replay and only interrupted by six minutes of commercials. (Advertising time in today's one-hour television program has nearly doubled in terms of commercial time per hour.) That is not enough time and space to present all the novel's suspicions, hearsay rumors, courtroom testimonies and circumstantial evidence. Under these conditions the public confession as spectacle rather than correct interpretation of circumstantial evidence becomes the climactic moment of truth and justice.

Admittedly, the outburst of a spectator that he or she committed the murder does not happen in everyday courtrooms. Suspending this completely fictional aspect, though, there is a striking problem with the confession. The confessor has heretofore been a witness, telling both the prosecution and defense his or her observations that indicate both personal innocence and reasons for believing Mason's client is guilty. Often the confessor knows the defendant, sometimes as a friend, colleague, even lover or family member. This intimacy does not deter the murderer from anticipating that the defendant—be it friend, colleague, even lover or family member—take the rap and is found guilty in the court of law.

After all, spectators must ask themselves: If the confessor has lied or deceived while being a witness—and so undeserving of our trust, on what basis is his or her confession now to be accepted as a true statement? Why should the confessional statement resolve a legal or moral battle when it is made by an untrustworthy person? Is there a qualitative difference between speaking falsehoods about others and speaking the truth about oneself, so that the truth about oneself is recognized by us as genuine rather than another ploy in perjury or disguise?

In the novel *The Case of the Half-Wakened Wife*, a philandering husband is murdered and his jealous wife becomes Mason's defendant. The eventual murderer is a greedy investor who defrauded the husband. The television version makes the wife the murderer due to her jealousy, anger and humiliation by means of her wayward husband. Whereas the

161

novel ends with the actual murderer proven in a private deposition, the television show culminates with the wife initiating an orgy of sensations. She becomes a spectacle of rage, heart-felt remorse, undying love, desperate hope that ushers in her dramatic and moving confession. Under such an orgy of conditions, the confession convinces—and entertains— judge, jury, courtroom spectators, and millions of television viewers.

Know thyself, encouraged Socrates. Beware of self-delusion, admonished Lao Tzu and Chuang Tzu. In its own way, the Perry Mason project brought to large audiences an enduring and appealing invitation to consider and enjoy witnessing other human being so ostensibly telling the truth about their own misdeeds and crimes.

## In the Name of Truth and Justice

... what they demanded was that the guilty party say something about his crime—that he say why he committed his crime, what meaning he gave to his gesture ...

—MICHEL FOUCAULT, *Wrong-Doing, Truth-Telling*, p. 21

This demand has become part of our cultural landscape. According to Michel Foucault, one of the pre-eminent thinkers of the twentieth century, confession (or avowal) has played a prominent role in a variety of moral, spiritual and legal domains since the ancient Greeks and early Christians. In more recent times this has expanded into psychiatry and criminal justice. Underscoring these roles is the moment an individual testifies to the truth about him- or herself and the unexpected response of the audience.

Many rituals of confession appear before a very limited or secretive audience. Telling of your alleged sins before a priest or suspected crimes before a torturer might force false statements about yourself. There are cases of individuals falsely admitting a crime in order to protect the guilty relative or friend. The act of telling about oneself to another presents a challenge and exercise in assessing the truthfulness of these self-accounts. Diotima gives Socrates the riddle that he is wisest because he knows that he does not know. For Foucault, that is only part of the story. Another part empha-

## "Yes! I Did It!"

sizes how we do know some things about ourselves, but to truly realize or understand them requires confessing this knowledge to others.

This task presents a conundrum. We can say that giraffes fly, 2 + 3 = 5, bachelors are married, or the sky is not blue, and we can readily verify the claims (or infer that the speaker is mad). How to determine whether the speaker is telling the truth about him- or herself precludes such independent verification. For we must first surmise some frame of reference and background knowledge about the speaker. In this light a confession presents a distinct problem in assessing whether claims about yourself are true or false.

Foucault traces the birth of this problem to the ancient Greeks and early Christian Fathers. They emphasized the concern and techniques to know oneself in order to be a good citizen or faithful follower of God. Addressing this problem has an ambivalent history, particularly as it crosses both private and public domains. There were traditions of confessing to your mentor or master, talking about dreams, ambitions, desires and inner thoughts in order to elicit an identify weaknesses and strengths of your self. There were also traditions in which confessions were forced through public ordeals and political tortures. The Roman spectacles, for example, indulged viewers with the suspense of a possible confession from the heretics about to be slaughtered by ferocious beasts. During medieval times it was a faithful executioner who inflicted his instruments of pain upon the criminal to elicit a possible final confession before a fascinated public.

How any of these moments demonstrates that confessions are true statements is resolved by an unpredictable but compelling dynamic. You confess to others—in an act that anticipates a response from others—in order to establish and ascertain the truth about yourself. The audience assesses how sincere, lucid, consistent, and factual the confession seems to be, and how it resonates with what is already known about the confessor.

In more recent times, contends Foucault, the act of confessing to being the author of a crime no longer suffices. In the context of criminal justice, the confession is expected to include an explanation of why and how you did the crime.

**Alexander E. Hooke**

The culprit must replay his past and articulate the darker passages of his soul. Justice cannot be fully administered until the court and the public learns the criminal's account of himself. The new drama is not an aftereffect or sidelight—it is essential to reaching the truth. In Foucault's words:

> If one understands the 'dramatic' not as a mere ornamental addition, but as every element in a scene that brings forth the foundation of legitimacy and the meaning of what is taking place, then I would say that confession (avowal) is part of the judicial and penal drama . . . The appetite for confession—the appetite for veridiction of the crime by its perpetrator—is central to our criminal investigation. (p. 210)

Perry Mason feeds this appetite. Intentionally or not, the television version entices spectators with a curiosity that is satisfied only upon learning who the culprit is and why he or she committed the murder.

For example, in "The Case of the Playboy Pugilist," viewers are presented with several witnesses—each a plausible suspect for the murder attributed to Mason's client, a boxer with very little talent. The murder victim is not a sympathetic figure—scam artist, hustler, lothario. He hustled the boxer's manager into signing a bogus contract. As always, the evidence against Mason's defendant seems insurmountable until, in this case, the victim was murdered by his mistress to whom he promised marriage. The mistress accidentally overheard him telephoning another woman with the same promise. She cries, bemoans her bad luck, berates her disloyal lover, vividly recalls her sacrifices in order to be with him—only to find that she was deceived, betrayed and abandoned. Yes, she did it. And here is why.

Another case finds an accountant allowing his wife to be the defendant for suspicion of murdering her boss. Mason tricks him into admitting that he has embezzled over $200,000 from the firm while doing its books. He confesses to the theft and being the actual murderer of the boss by laughing about his outsmarting everyone for all those years. One television confessor pathetically weeps before the audience saying his heinous deed can be attributed to his wife of twenty years who always nagged and berated him. Some confessors apologize to the defendants or regret their rash decision, while others admit they are glad to have killed the malevolent victim and would easily do it again.

In any event, the confession—made by someone who throughout the story has proven to be a liar—is accepted as true. And its truthfulness is demonstrated not so much by the correct interpretation of the evidence, as emphasized in the Perry Mason novels, but by the drama in which the confession unfolds. With the passions, conflicting testimonies, conniving strategies and empathetic characters that comprise this drama, the audience is treated to a legal spectacle fostered by a public confession. In contrast to the accuracy of the scientific objectivity of forensics, the truth of spectacle confession is anchored by what Foucault calls "criminal subjectivity"—the acknowledgement of the deed and a description or explanation of the criminal's own self.

The television spectacle of confession is fictional. No one attending a real court hearing experiences a person suddenly standing among the spectators to shout, "Yes, I did it!" Yet this objection overlooks two points. One, all spectacles rely on an element of fiction. From ancient Roman amphitheaters to modern sports arenas, spectacles are enlivened by the various stories surrounding them. Two, this element contributes to the variety of sensations comprising the confession that is judged to be true or false. These two points underscore the enduring influence of the Perry Mason phenomenon.

## For All to See

> The audience out front sees only the carefully rehearsed poses assumed by the actors. The lawyer sees human nature with the shutters open.
>
> —PERRY MASON, in *The Case of the Caretaker's Cat*

In his novels Erle Stanley Gardner occasionally writes a detailed and eloquent dedication to specific police officials or criminal justice researchers he met and who are committed to deploying the most current methods of forensic science, or what Gardner called legal medicine. For example, *The Case of the Worried Waitress* gives readers a sense of Gardner's admiration for Marshall Houts, investigator for the Court of

Last Resort, and Don Harper Mills, an MD practicing forensic medicine in Los Angeles, for embracing and furthering the importance of the most recent discoveries that help determine innocence of those wrongfully convicted of murder and the guilt of those lawbreakers who have so far have eluded justice.

Forensics and the confession share two more features. Both are public events; the etymology of forensics stems from "forum"—to make an open demonstration of your interpretation of the evidence with others having the opportunity to challenge it. They also share a common adversary—the eyewitness.

A notoriously uneven figure in determining the truth of a crime, the eyewitness to an alleged crime has historically been a controversial cornerstone of criminal proceedings. Numerous studies in the history of forensics invariably address how unreliable, if not dishonest or treacherous, eyewitness reports can be. A spate of recent books, such as *The Killer of Little Shepherds, The Faithful Executioner*, and *Silent Witnesses*, have examined the gradual need for more scientific alternatives to the central role of eyewitnesses who can betray truth and justice with their mendacity, spite, slopping memory, treacherous motives, and inept misstatements. Legal medicine, in Gardner's words, is the better friend of truth and justice.

The confession poses a different type of adversary to the eyewitness. Unlike forensics, which relies on experts to interpret objective facts and impartial evidence to piece together the crime, the confession provides a subjective component that is fundamental to the juridical and public involvement in establishing and ascertaining the veracity of the confession. Scientifically proven facts do not suffice—we also need the drama of the criminal's own account so we can enjoy the suspense and judge its veracity at the same time. Eyewitness testimony lacks this sort of spectacle.

While the Perry Mason novels more noticeably embrace the advances in forensics, the television shows thrive on the confession. Many current crime shows (*Bones* being the most obvious) rely on the latest developments in forensics. But the public confession—from celebrity and political scandals to

### "Yes! I Did It!"

everyday entertainment—attracts vaster attention. It offers all viewers a chance to partake in the drama and determine the possible moment of truth. For in such spectacles, we catch a glimpse of human nature with the shutters open.

# 15
# Judge Not, Lest You . . .

ALEXANDER E. HOOKE

> Listen, you judges! There is another madness as well; and it comes *before* the deed. Ah, you have not crept deep enough into this soul!
>
> —FRIEDRICH NIETZSCHE, "On the Pale Criminal," *Thus Spoke Zarathustra*

Spectators, witnesses, and reporters shuffle through the main door of the courtroom. The bailiff enters from a side door to remind the audience about respecting protocol and procedure in order for justice to be properly administered. Then the jury enters from another side door while prosecutor Hamilton Burger and defense attorney Perry Mason with his client approach their respective front tables. The bailiff returns and in a booming voice announces, "All Rise!"

Everyone stands as a black-robed figure enters the courtroom and promptly climbs the steps to the solemn chair atop the bench, as if a sacral priest has just ascended the altar. He then gazes down upon the audience and quickly surveys the scene. He casts a glance at the lawyers ready to make their case. The judge has arrived and the trial is about to begin. It is judgment day, a day when someone in the room will be reckoning with his or her guilt before all these people.

The black-robed figure is not the only judge in this scene. The jurors, by weighing the evidence and testimony as fairly and objectively as possible, have the official duty as peers and of the accused to make a rational verdict. After watching the proceedings and adversarial tactics of the lawyers, the courtroom's spectators have likely taken sides and await the jury to confirm their choice. There is also the judgment that comes from outside the courtroom—the local public that might follow the trial through news reports or word-of-mouth, observations from neighbors, friends, or colleagues. In the case of Perry Mason's novel readers and screen viewers, the number of judges jumps into the millions.

According to Friedrich Nietzsche, the power and function of judgment—be it moral, legal, aesthetic, political—does not exist in the animal world. Animals make decisions, they attack and defend, they communicate and feel pleasure and pain, but they do not judge one another. They do not establish a separate space and time in which members of our own species debate another member's merits and qualities, deliberate the kinds of punishments deserved for the wrong-doer, uphold rules and symbols of justice that demand obedience, and establish a hierarchy of figures who are responsible for seeing that justice is done. Judgment is a human endeavor, or, in Nietzsche's more ambivalent tone, an all-too-human endeavor.

This ambivalence often arises when reading or watching a Perry Mason case. Audiences understandably enjoy the struggle of forces between good/bad or right/wrong, seeking assurance that justice will be served. They are fascinated by the variety of characters and surprise twists of the unfolding story. On the one hand, you (or he, she, me, we—any spectator) feel repulsed when hearing of the gruesome murder, the details about the bloody stabbing, grim drowning, or cold-hearted gunshots.

On the other hand, as the plot develops and various potential suspects appear, we develop a momentary affinity for the criminal. We did not like the victim either. More importantly, like the accused, most of us have encountered similar situations. At one time or another we felt cheated, desperate, greedy, vengeful, jealous, humiliated, backed into a corner with few resources, and unable to solve our problems through legitimate channels.

But you and I stopped short of committing a horrible deed. We did not resort to murder. In the following pages we attempt to address the following dilemma: Whereas Perry Mason untangles the logical path of the murderer by appealing to readers and viewers (as well as potential jurors) to imagine themselves in the murderer's situation, the path reaches an inherent dead end. At some point the murderer did what you and I could not do, as if we eluded the momentary madness of the misdeed.

The background to this issue does not only pertain to the courtroom. Ours is a culture of judgment. Political dramas, social media, news scandals, and popular entertainment thrive on the disparate pleasures humans experience when judging one another. The Perry Mason project provides an opportunity to address several features of judgment and its ambivalence in human life.

## Means, Motive, Opportunity

Perry Mason often likens solving a case to completing a complex jigsaw puzzle. Just as some of the pieces are hard to fit in, surprising facts of the case momentarily undermine the lawyer's hypothesis or plans for a successful defense. To figure out the keys to the crime Mason has to assume there are rational components to the murder. This assumption relies on three central themes—means, motive and opportunity.

Proving murder in the first degree requires the prosecution to demonstrate to the jury and judge that the defendant was quite capable to carrying out the deed, had an obvious moment when he or she could commit the heinous act while safely avoiding suspicion, and had strong reasons or expressed intense emotions against the murder victim. Each theme is essential to the drama and legal battle.

If the defendant lacked the strength, money, know-how, or tools to commit a particular murder, then he is too incompetent or ignorant to have murdered and must be acquitted. If it can be established that the defendant was somewhere else at the time of the murder, then she has an established alibi and must be found not guilty. And if the defendant may have some serious issues with her corrupt friend, his impossible boss, his cheating wife, her philandering husband, the town's billionaire bully, a terrifying neighbor, Mason will plead to the jury and judge to look and assess his client—an object of wrongful accusation in which the evidence clearly shows the defendant simply has no reason to murder.

In sum, there are three types of adversarial relations underscoring the courtroom drama:

**Means vs. Incompetence or Ignorance**

**Opportunity vs. Alibi**

and

**Motive vs. No Malice**

Erle Stanley Gardner, the creator of Perry Mason, used his considerable experience as a trial lawyer in California to devise numerous scenarios where Mason operates and thrives on these adversarial relations.

In *The Case of the Mischievous Doll,* the defendant is accused of murder via purposeful vehicle attack upon the victim. The story itself is a bit convoluted, as it involves the defendant disguising herself. She believes she is being framed for murder of a woman who is actually supposed to be her. Obviously frightened and confused, she alters her identity to avoid suspicion while seeking legal counsel. In an odd twist, she becomes both the murder victim and the murderer. Mason gets his faithful detective Paul Drake and loyal secretary Della Street to keep their eyes open and tell him what he doesn't see. He then learns his client's real identity. Finally, he puts the timeline of the sequence of events, incorporates key findings of Drake and Street, then highlights inaccuracies and contradictions in the testimony of witnesses and submitted evidence. His client, the defendant, could not have been at the scene of the crime. Alibi.

It is actually quite difficult to kill someone by driving a car and have no one find out. It takes special skill to drive into someone once and be sure of the victim's death. Cars leave all sorts of evidence for detectives—skid marks, broken glass, blood on the car's exterior, fresh dents from bumping into a tree or telephone pole. The defendant has no such abilities. Incompetence or Ignorance.

For the clincher, Mason then demonstrates that the fingerprints of the alleged victim and his defendant are identical. Chief investigator Lieutenant Tragg and prosecutor Hamilton Burger are stunned by the surprise. Mason looks

## Judge Not, Lest You . . .

to them and, with the smirk of a victor, asks the court on what basis can his defendant be tried for killing herself. No Malice.

And no conviction—Mason wins again. As a favor to the prosecution and the jury, Mason quickly points to the actual murderer sitting in the courtroom, who then leaps towards the exit door only to be apprehended by the guards.

Mason also relies on the means/motive/opportunity theme to find the culprit. In *The Case of the Angry Mourner* Mason is faced with a potentially tragic strategy. His client, mother of a young, smart, and attractive woman, is accused of murder as a response to aggressive advances of a wealthy and wheelchair-bound bachelor made towards her daughter. He's a notorious womanizer and keeps expensive items in the house. So there is also suspicion of romantic revenge or burglary. Mason's client and her daughter live a couple of hundred yards from the victim.

The tragic aspect is that there is considerable suspicion of the daughter being the murderer and the mother is willing to take the blame. In this light, Mason can defend his client by showing the daughter to be the actual killer. Or he can force the daughter to testify by providing the jury sufficient evidence to find her own mother guilty.

Two of the key witnesses are husband and wife neighbors who are quite nosy and gossipy. In the middle of the night he hears a loud noise—a scream, crash, or possible gun shot. She has a telescope (binoculars in the television show) strong enough to see at a distance in the dimly lit neighborhood. They tell prosecutors they spotted the mother running from the victim's house. The wife even speculates that both daughter and mother are separately making romantic overtures to the same wealthy murder victim. The spectator quickly comes upon the murder scene. Victim slumped in wheelchair, blood trickling out of his mouth. Shattered dishware, lipstick on a glass, a woman's compact that the mother knew was a birthday present from the victim to her daughter.

Mason soon suspects the husband. From private investigators and his own research, Mason learns the husband has motive, means, and opportunity. The husband grew up in the country and knew how to create and erase foot tracks in sand, frosty grounds, and mud, key evidence in terms of the defendant's own movements. The husband was the only one awake during the entire scenario, and anticipated the defendant might visit the victim one of these nights. He staged the murder to show that it looked like the daughter did it while realizing the mother would arrive to rearrange the murder scene to deflect official attention to her daughter.

The scheme almost worked. But Mason detected one or two minor but significant flaws in the husband's report while soon learning the motive. The victim had exploited the real murderer's financial stake in the area, and husband resented the humiliating defeat and the futility of his own future due to his financial miscalculations. If you read the first couple of chapters of this novel (the television version does not show this), the motive is clearly introduced. The murderer already tells his wife of his hatred of the victim and that maybe "one of these girls gave him (the victim) what he had coming."

A shameful confession—in my first encounter with *The Case of the Angry Mourner* I never suspected the husband.

## Suspense

Essential to most popular crime entertainment is the eventual identification of the real culprit. The satisfaction that an innocent human being might have been protected by Mason from an unjust destiny of jail or execution rarely suffices for a crime story to be successful in television, movies, and novels. Audiences prefer the additional suspense of "I knew he was the real murderer" or "I would never guess she could have done such a terrible thing."

This double-suspense, the twists and turns of the plot and characters as well as the "whodunnit" are fundamental to the popular and enduring life of a crime genre venture. Erle Stanley Gardner, after several rejections of his crime writings, landed a remarkable success with his Perry Mason project. It sold around three hundred million copies. Translated into more than a dozen languages, the Perry Mason project was represented and reinvented through radio broadcasts, a top-ten television program for nine years, and several movies.

For Gardner, this double-suspense had to retain realistic characters and plots. Too much fantasy or science-fiction

### Judge Not, Lest You . . .

might entertain the audience with spectacular imagery, but at the risk of an audience not stimulated by the intellectual and emotional task of making a possible judgment on the guilt or innocence of a fellow human being. Many masters of the crime story genre began their chapters as serial short versions in crime magazines. The magazines were inexpensive and timely spaced between issues so fans could debate the next courtroom scene of likely culprit, much like today's audiences assessing likely winners and losers for football playoffs, March Madness in college basketball, or the latest trendy television drama. After Gardner triumphed over these early literary trials and tribulations, he nevertheless always fretted that his stories were becoming predictable or that he had exhausted all the courtroom twists and turns. God forbid that Perry Mason becomes boring!

Gardner refused to cave in to charges of "boring!" by developing a romance between Perry and Della. After he ceased legal practices, he began volunteering his services and expertise to a national forum that tried to select candidates who needed and deserved free legal support. This helped him to stay updated about latest advances in forensics (what he called "legal medicine") in terms of methods and technologies. The cases he studied reminded his cynical side of the ever-creative ways humans commit crime while eluding the grips of justice. Partly what must have sustained his interest in the Perry Mason project was the fascination of human judgment—particularly when it came to judging one another.

## The Judging Animal

> Perhaps our word "man" (manas) still expresses something of precisely *this* feeling of self-satisfaction: man, designated himself as the creature that measures values, evaluates and measures, as the "valuating animal as such."
>
> —FRIEDRICH NIETZSCHE, *Genealogy of Morals*, II/8

Judgment is more than merely expressing a taste or preference. To judge someone or something involves relying on criteria, information, standards, and background. The scientist evaluates the accuracy of a hypothesis by conducting experiments and sorting out significant and relevant data. Judges in talent shows or Olympic events have an array of measurements from their experiences, trained eyes and background knowledge to assess whether the performer deserves a 9.2 or 9.5 out of a possible 10. The doctor determines what the X-rays or MRI results mean for the patient's immediate or long-term prognosis.

Judging another human being's motives and actions involves a different kind of evaluation. Numbers and precise criteria are less helpful. To ascertain someone being good or evil, virtuous or vicious, innocent or guilty, a contributor or corrupter of the common good, our valuations are no longer guided primarily by independent factors. For Nietzsche, judging others invariably involves an element of judging ourselves—or misjudging ourselves. Am I not better than the accused miscreant? There is an element of self-satisfaction rather than objective inquiry when contemplating this question.

In this light we now address Gardner admitting to a defect after publishing the first two Perry Mason novels. He worried that the books can "show the facts leading up to the crime, and then the solution comes in the courtroom." In other words, the connection or transition between "crime facts" and "courtroom solution" seemed awkward or absent. Being the first crime writer to emphasize courtroom battles, Gardner was unsure how to strike a balance between the various appeals offered in pulp fiction and the lofty expectations of intellectual readers who preferred the aesthetic and logic of a "whodunnit." According to Gardner biographer Dorothy Hughes, the Mason novels were geared to a thoughtful reader who is on plane, a tired doctor or frustrated lawyer, maybe an exhausted teacher or leisurely vacationer looking for some engaging books. They want the stimulation of a puzzling drama, but they also want an entertaining, lively and concise read.

In our view, Gardner's self-critique does not encompass a defect. To the contrary, this alleged defect can be construed as a gap or intellectual space that entices the reader or viewer to deliberate the possible connections between the "crime facts" and the "courtroom solution." Fans of seeing Perry Mason in action are treated to a variety of courtroom dramas that are not typical of how we relate to people in everyday circumstances. The courtroom is run by officials and professionals. The presiding judge determines who can speak and when. The attorneys exchange fanciful jargon such as immaterial and irrelevant, leading the witness, violation of legal code, even speaking some esoteric language like Latin. Jury members are silent. Any interruption among the spectators will lead to expulsion from the courtroom.

On the "crime facts" side, by contrast, audiences are already familiar with an array of sundry witnesses, gossipers, malcontents, grudge-holders, and salacious suspects. The suspicions and rumors are the stuff of everyday life and common speech. Before the defendant ever sits before the judge and jury, Perry Mason audiences are already sifting through clues and reports that surround the case. They see traces of greed, revenge, and greed, and recall cursing, slang and speech uncontrolled by court protocol. They detect anger, resentment, and duplicity that might be difficult to demonstrate before a jury. They quickly form views about the beautiful and seductive young woman, snarling millionaire, spoiled playboy, betrayed lover, or sniveling but sneaky neighbor. We evaluate the suspects with all-too-human eyes.

Shifting to the courtroom solution, Perry Mason's millions of fans are suddenly potential jurors. Here their perception is differently shaped. No gossip or hearsay, no gut feelings or intuitions are allowed. Matters before the court are decided by the judge as parlayed through the attorneys. Judgments in the courtroom have completely different parameters than those formed in ordinary life. This gap or intellectual space that bothered Gardner, we contend, could well be the source that energized and guided the Perry Mason project's enduring appeal. When learning of the myriad facts of the crime as discovered in police reports, newspaper items, investigators' questions, the audience has the chance to anticipate and deliberate how the courtroom proceedings will unfold, and, of course, how Mason's client will be found not guilty.

## You, Me, and the Criminal

A brief but telling glimpse from *The Case of the Silent Partner*. Perry Mason confides to Della Street his suspicions of a shady witness to the crime attributed to his client. Della objects, "But you don't even *know* him, Chief." Mason responds that you don't always need face-to-face encounters. He asserts that with careful observation, particularly by trying to scrutinize the target through the eyes of others, lots can be learned. Della then raises the problem that people often see things through a bias or prejudice.

Mason's rejoinder is striking. "You make allowances for that prejudice when you know the others. You can then judge the extent of their distortion. That's the only way you can solve cases, Della. You must learn to know the characters involved. You must learn to see things through their eyes, and that means you *must have sympathy and tolerance for crime*" (Emphasis in original).

This is not about being hard or soft on crime. Sympathy and tolerance refer to how characters in a murder plot understand—maybe even not begrudge—the actions of a potential murderer. Mason's talents manifest not only in his knowledge of the law and courtroom tactics—but as an acute observer of humans viewing other humans.

Perry Mason realizes that when judging another person's guilt or innocence before the law, we are assessing not just the physical actions. We are, in Nietzsche's words, peering into and judging another's soul. And few of us can creep deep enough to detect the trace of madness that came before the deed.

# 16
# Justice: The Master Narrative

CRAIG R. CHRISTIANSEN

A Perry Mason book or TV episode is not simply description, it is action. It teaches, explains, and demonstrates meaning through specific actions—it is a narrative. We understand Perry Mason as part of a *master* narrative that is so prevalent in our society that it seems to be just 'common sense'— the legal process is a search, not simply for truth, but for justice.

The essential story line of each story does not develop around the accused, but rather around the actions of an advocate for justice. While Perry's explicit goal is assumed to be winning the case for his client, his actions often serve as commentary or critique of essential elements of the legal system. In fact, for much of the English-speaking world, the stories of Perry Mason are an important gateway in coming to understand the legal process. But the narrative is not about the legal skills of Perry Mason, it is about the search for justice—which does not *necessarily* mean an acquittal for Perry's client.

If you were asked to identify the central character in the Perry Mason books or TV episodes, what would be your answer? What, after all, is the story about? Aristotle's view was that the play is not about the characters, but about the action—the behavior of humans towards one another. So, let's not focus on the personality of Perry Mason, but rather, explore *how* he seeks justice—and understands the boundaries of the legal system that is his stage. Those boundaries are the assumptions of the Master Narrative of justice.

Craig R. Christiansen

## The Master Narrative

There are always alternative stories, but generally only one predominant, or "master" story about important understandings of our life-world. The great social biologist E.O. Wilson writes, "Human beings *must* [my emphasis] have an epic, a sublime account of how the world was created and how humanity became part of it . . ." These stories can be fantastic or scientific. Most are deeply rooted in history and culture.

For instance, every religious tradition has a creation story that forms an important part of the sense that particular belief system makes of our world. For the Judeo-Christian tradition, that is the story of Adam and Eve. It explains the creation of the world, of humankind, the relationship with God, and the ongoing attempt to recapture the paradise the original humans once had.

Even atheists are familiar with the creation story of Adam and Eve. Both the story and its elements are part of our common language. Of course, there are counter-narratives, such as the Big Bang theory, Darwin's theory of evolution, the Norse Yggdrasil, the Hopi sipapu, the Hindu Brahma, and countless others, but the story of Adam and Eve remains as a common theme in modern America. It is a Master Narrative.

So, what are the elements of our story . . . our Master Narrative . . . on Justice? Our first responses might deal with such topics as fairness, appropriateness, uniformity, feasibility, or authority. Or we might tell the story centered on the purpose of justice: revenge or retribution, restoration or rehabilitation. It may even center on the distribution of the law among classes or between citizens and non-citizens. Historically, all of these topics have once held prominence in ideas of justice.

As we look at two of Perry Mason's many cases, we can see how his search for justice confronts two issues.

## The Call to Care and Responsibility

"The Case of the Substitute Face" involves the Houser family that Della Street and Perry met on board a ship. Conspicuous travelers include a nurse escorting a patient with a completely bandaged face. Mrs. Houser tells Perry Mason that

# Bibliography

Arendt, Hannah. 1963, *Eichmann in Jerusalem: A Report on the Banality of Evil.* Viking.
———. 1972. Thinking and Moral Considerations. In Kohn 1972.
Aristotle. 1987. *Poetics.* Hackett.
Bataille, Georges, Isabelle Waldberg, and Iain White. 1995. *Encyclopaedia Acephalica: Comprising the Critical Dictionary and Related Texts.* Atlas.
Bierce, Ambrose. 2002. *The Unabridged Devil's Dictionary.* University of Georgia Press.
Blanchot, Maurice, and Jacques Derrida. 2000. *The Instant of My Death. / Demeure: Fiction and Testimony.* Stanford University Press.
Bok, Sissela. 1997. *Secrets.* Viking.
Bounds, J. Dennis. 1996. *Perry Mason: The Authorship and Reproduction of a Popular Hero.* Praeger.
Braccialarghe, Randolph. 2004. Why Were Perry Mason's Clients Always Innocent? The Criminal Lawyer's Moral Dilemma—The Criminal Defendant Who Tells His Lawyer He Is Guilty. *Valparaiso University Law Review* 39:1 (Fall).
Brightman, Carol, ed. 1996. *Between Friends: The Correspondence of Hannah Arendt and Mary McCarthy, 1949–1975.* Harcourt Brace.
Brown, Dan. 2009 [2003]. *The Da Vinci Code.* Anchor.
Confucius. 2002. *The Analects.* The Chinese University Press.
Crombag, H.F.M., W.A. Wagenaar, and P.J. van Koppen. 1996. Crashing Memories and the Problem of 'Source Monitoring'. *Applied Cognitive Psychology* 10.
Derrida, Jacques. 1992. The Force of Law: The Mystical Foundations of Authority. *Cardozo Law Review* 11.

## Bibliography

———. 1999. *Adieu to Emmanuel Levinas*. Stanford University Press.
Foucault, Michel. 1988. *Technologies of the Self: A Seminar with Michel Foucault*. University of Massachusetts Press.
———. 2014. *Wrong-Doing, Truth-Telling*. University of Chicago Press.
Fugate, Francis L., and Roberta B. Fugate. 2015. *Secrets of the World's Best-Selling Writer: The Storytelling Technique of Erle Stanley Gardner*. Graymalkin.
Gardner, Erle Stanley. 1944. The Greatest Detectives I Know. *McClurg Book News* (January–February).
———. 1945. Explaining Headless Murders. *The American Weekly* (October 14th).
———. 1945. Is This the Perfect Crime? *The American Weekly* (October 21st).
———. 1946. The Case of the Movie Murder. *True* (June).
———. 1946. The Case of the Early Beginning. In Haycraft 1946.
———. 1947. The Case of the Red-Headed Killer. *True Police Cases* (May).
———. 1948. How I Came to Create Perry Mason. *Lintas Proprietary*.
———. 1949. Democracy by Dissent. *This Week* (October 2nd).
———. 1950. Circumstantial Evidence in Homicide Cases. *Michigan State Bar Journal* (November).
———. 1952. Should Justice Be Blind? *Civic Forum*, University of Miami (May).
———. 1952. Beware the Eye-Witness. *The American Weekly* (August 17th).
———. 1952. *The Court of Last Resort*. Morrow.
———. 1954. *Neighborhood Frontiers*. Morrow.
———. 1955. Can We Cope with Crime? *Fortnight* (December 1955–February 1956).
———. 1955. *The Case of the Guilty Client*. Texas Bar Association.
———. 1958. Confessions of a Cross-Examiner. *Journal of Forensic Sciences* (July).
———. 1959. The Many Meanings an 'Escape' Novel Holds for Its Many Readers. *New York Herald Tribune* (January 18th).
———. 1960. *Hunting the Desert Whale*. Morrow.
———. 1961. *Hovering over Baja*. Morrow.
———. 1962. *The Hidden Heart of Baja*. Morrow.
———. 1963. *The Desert Is Yours*. Morrow.
———. 1964. *The World of Water*. Morrow.
———. 1965. Getting Away with Murder. *Atlantic Monthly* (January).
———. 1965. Who Is Perry Mason? *Chicago Daily News* (October 2nd).

### The Classic TV Episodes

20. The Case of the Poison Pen-Pal"
21. "The Case of the Mystified Miner"
22. "The Case of the Crippled Cougar"
23. "The Case of the Absent Artist"
24. "The Case of the Melancholy Marksman"
25. "The Case of the Angry Astronaut"
26. "The Case of the Borrowed Baby"
27. "The Case of the Counterfeit Crank"
28. "The Case of the Ancient Romeo"
29. "The Case of the Promoter's Pillbox"
30. "The Case of the Lonely Eloper"

## Season Six (1962-63)

1. "The Case of the Bogus Books"
2. "The Case of the Capricious Corpse"
3. "The Case of the Playboy Pugilist"
4. "The Case of the Double-Entry Mind"
5. "The Case of the Hateful Hero"
6. "The Case of the Dodging Domino"
7. "The Case of the Unsuitable Uncle"
8. "The Case of the Stand-In Sister"
9. "The Case of the Weary Watchdog"
10. "The Case of the Lurid Letter"
11. "The Case of the Fickle Filly"
12. "The Case of the Polka-Dot Pony"
13. "The Case of the Shoplifter's Shoe"
14. "The Case of the Bluffing Blast"
15. "The Case of the Prankish Professor"
16. "The Case of Constant Doyle"
17. "The Case of the Libelous Locket"
18. "The Case of the Two-Faced Turnabout"
19. "The Case of the Surplus Suitor"
20. "The Case of the Golden Oranges"
21. "The Case of the Lawful Lazarus"
22. "The Case of the Velvet Claws"
23. "The Case of the Lover's Leap"
24. "The Case of the Elusive Element"
25. "The Case of the Greek Goddess"
26. "The Case of the Skeleton's Closet"
27. "The Case of the Potted Planter"

28. "The Case of the Witless Witness"

## Season Seven (1963-64)

1. "The Case of the Nebulous Nephew"
2. "The Case of the Shifty Shoebox"
3. "The Case of the Drowsy Mosquito"
4. "The Case of the Deadly Verdict"
5. "The Case of the Decadent Dean"
6. "The Case of the Reluctant Model"
7. "The Case of the Bigamous Spouse"
8. "The Case of the Floating Stones"
9. "The Case of the Festive Felon"
10. "The Case of the Devious Delinquent"
11. "The Case of the Bouncing Boomerang"
12. "The Case of the Badgered Brother"
13. "The Case of the Wednesday Woman"
14. "The Case of the Accosted Accountant"
15. "The Case of the Capering Camera"
16. "The Case of the Ice-Cold Hands"
17. "The Case of the Bountiful Beauty"
18. "The Case of the Nervous Neighbor"
19. "The Case of the Fifty-Millionth Frenchman"
20. "The Case of the Frightened Fisherman"
21. "The Case of the Arrogant Arsonist"
22. "The Case of the Garrulous Go-Between"
23. "The Case of the Woeful Widower"
24. "The Case of the Simple Simon"
25. "The Case of the Illicit Illusion"
26. "The Case of the Antic Angel"
27. "The Case of the Careless Kidnapper"
28. "The Case of the Drifting Dropout"
29. "The Case of the Tandem Target"
30. "The Case of the Ugly Duckling"

## Season Eight (1964-65)

1. "The Case of the Missing Button"
2. "The Case of the Paper Bullets"
3. "The Case of the Scandalous Sculptor"
4. "The Case of the Sleepy Slayer

# Index

Alder, Dianne, 14–18
alibi, 69, 111, 157, 172
Allison, Norda, 17
Anthony, Casey, vii
Aquinas, St. Thomas, 27, 30
Arendt, Hannah, 41–46, 183, 187, 189, 191
Aristotle, 30, 145–155, 189

Bagby, Evelyn, 82
Bayes's Theorem, 82–89
Bayes, Reverend Thomas, 81
belief, 3, 29, 64–66, 72–73, 84, 88, 96, 120, 122, 125, 180, 187
Becker, Alfred, 188
Benedict, Nathan, 17
Blake, Robert, vii
Boring, Harrison T., 14–22
Burger, Hamilton, 65–73, 76– 80, 115–16, 121–22, 160, 169, 172
Burr, Raymond, 111, 115, 128, 153, 192, 197

Caddo, Robert, 97, 135–9
Carroll, Lewis, 30
categorical imperative, 11
catharsis, 154

CBS, 44
character (psychological personality), 133, 137–150
characterization, 33–34, 150–51
climax (literary device), 147–48
conditional probability, 82
confession, 7, 35–36, 72, 77, 88, 93, 100, 148, 151, 154, 158–59 161–66, 174
Confucius, 16–18
culpability, 29–31

*The Da Vinci Code*, 95
deduction, 75–79
defense, 75–77
defense mechanism, 127
deontology, 13, 21
denial, 43, 127
discovery, 119, 147–48
displacement, 127
DNA evidence, vii, 49–62
Dostoyevski, Fyodor, 31
Drake, Paul, ix, 24–25, 73, 87, 93, 107, 109, 113–17, 120, 129–130, 137, 140, 153, 172
Eichmann, Adolf, 38–42
*Eichmann in Jerusalem*, 43
egoism, vii, 109–110, 134
Epicureanism, 14

# Index

ethics:
  equal with moral philosophy, 3, 11, 16, 18, 133
  ethical dilemmas and, 6, 12–25
  god and, 20, 95–98, 162
  legal profession and, 18–21, 31, 87, 103
  Perry Mason's struggle with, 6–10, 19–20
  virtue and, 17, 137, 162
evidence, 49–62, 63–74, 75–80, 81–90, 95, 101, 121–23, 125, 134–37, 140, 149, 157–161, 169–173, 184–86
evil
  actions and, 24, 112, 152
  banality and, 41–43
  lawyers and, vii
  problem of, 36, 46, 184
eyewitness evidence, 49–61, 122, 166
exoneration, viii, 49–61, 155
Ezekiel, 97

false accusation, 49–61
false memory, 49–61
female perspective, 133–141
feminism, 133–41
Fifth Amendment, 72, 126
Foster, Montrose, 17–18
Freud, Sigmund, 127

Gardner, Erle Stanley, vii, 14, 15, 21–23, 51, 60–61, 78, 100, 108–114, 119, 126, 129, 137, 140, 148, 150, 157, 159–160, 165–66, 172–77, 190, 193
Gestapo, 22
God, 95–98, 103–04, 152, 158, 163
god's-eye point of view, 29–31
Goodman, Saul, 27–34
Greek tragedy, 145–156
guilt; *see* innocence and guilt

Hale, Barbara, ix, 111, 204

Hayyoth, 97
Hobbes, Thomas, 27, 30
honesty, 8, 19–20, 55
Hughes, Dorothy, 176
Hughes, H. Stuart, 125–130
Hume, David, 63–64, 77, 79–80

induction, 75–79
induction vs. deduction, 75–79
innocence and guilt, 6, 19, 23–24, 50–51, 63–66, 83–86, 89, 105, 121, 148, 161, 166, 175, 178
The Innocence Project, viii, 50
Inquisition, The, 98

Jesus, 95–96, 103–05
Judas, 95
Judge Kent, 11
justice, 8–10, 15–18, 27–29, 30–34, 39, 61, 88, 95–100, 103–05, 133–14, 141, 149–150, 162–65, 179–188
justice system, 6, 30–31
justification, 65–67, 120
justified true belief, 65–67, 120

Kant, Immanuel, 4–5, 16, 18, 21–22, 27, 30

*The Last Supper*, 96, 103–04
law:
  and authority, 30
  and cases, vii
  and the Constitution, vii
  and a god or gods, 30
  and Lady Liberty, vii
lawyers
  arguing in the courtroom and, 6, 61, 119–132
  corruption and, vii, 33
  duty and, 9, 24, 116, 121
  laws and, 6, 116
  legal positivism, 27–34
Loftus, Elizabeth, 56–57